"The rise of the global church has [...] to be more culturally diverse than [...] teams are confronted with a new set of realities that test and challenge their prior assumptions about mission leadership. This book shares the honest stories of various vulnerable mission teams, the struggles they faced, and the lessons they learned in the process. *Teamwork Cross-Culturally* redefines mission, not just as a project to be accomplished but as a place where all involved need to learn and demonstrate a kingdom lifestyle through a radical pursuit of unity amid diversity. Thus, the book recenters discipleship as an ongoing need for those involved in missions. Anybody seeking to effectively and meaningfully participate in missions in the twenty-first century should read this book."

—**Michel Kenmogne**, SIL International

"Learning about intercultural communication is extremely important, but those who work with culturally diverse teams know that something deeper is also required. This book unpacks how and why leaning into the sacrificial message of the cross, abiding in Christ, and heeding Jesus's call for unity are so essential. These can be uncomfortable concepts for people who might prefer to focus on their rights, power, and privileges. Yet through a variety of passages, the authors illustrate biblical truths that create ways forward despite how complex and challenging diverse team situations can be!"

—**Mary T. Lederleitner**, author of *Cross-Cultural Partnerships* and *Women in God's Mission*

"This book represents the culmination of almost three decades of cross-cultural missiology in the Lingenfelter oeuvre, at least with respect to confronting in depth the 'wicked' or in principle irresolvable problems of ministering, teaching, and leading across ethnic, national, and cultural divides. The resolution is derived, at least in part and appropriately so given Lingenfelter's mentoring commitments and capacities, from one of his doctoral-students-turned-colleague, Julie Green. Across these pages, Lingenfelter and Green help us discern and name such wicked problems and give perspective on their negotiation and amelioration achievable only 'in Christ,' which enables forward organizational movement without being threatened by what may happen when we otherwise avoid what cannot be simply managed."

—**Amos Yong**, Fuller Theological Seminary

"Although written for cross-cultural team leaders and leaders of mission organizations, this remarkable book is helpful for all Christian leaders who are involved in multicultural churches or other organizations. It contains clarity about the problems we encounter with multicultural leadership, and it offers good, solid biblical and theological guidance in moving forward."

—**Scott W. Sunquist**, Gordon-Conwell Theological Seminary

"A much-needed look at the challenges and opportunities of multinational ministry teams in twenty-first-century missions. Lingenfelter and Green bring great experience and solid research to this work that builds on Jesus's metaphors of shepherd, servant, and steward as the goal for leaders in every cultural context. In-depth case studies present leaders who represent distinct styles of leadership and are working within different mission organizations in different regions of the world. But all are similarly tackling the complicated problems inherent in doing God's mission on multicultural teams. Lingenfelter and Green are unflinchingly honest about the temptation of leaders to use authority and power for control. Interpersonal relationship issues are painfully common. But the authors offer substantive hope by presenting strategies that can help teams forge unity of purpose, Jesus-like nurturing leadership, and members that value and learn from one another on the redemptive journey. For cross-cultural missionaries and leaders fulfilling God's mission in today's complex world, *Teamwork Cross-Culturally* is a valuable gift."

—**Beth Grant**, Assemblies of God

"In this missiological gem, Lingenfelter and Green illustrate how not all problems are created equal. Some problems are wicked! Such problems are never fully solved and frequently resist management solutions and common sense. In fact, they demand clumsy solutions, something the authors demonstrate convincingly through their compelling wisdom. They conclude that there is no single pathway to resolve the inevitable challenges of people from diverse nations and cultures working together. But by using redeemed power and leaning into cultural models and frames with cruciform identity and Christocentric cultural intelligence, we can develop a godly clumsiness that can effectively engage these wicked problems. *Teamwork Cross-Culturally* is not a how-to manual but rather a resource that will enable global servants to see their challenges through new theoretical and theological lenses. Chock-full of compelling case studies and penetrating analysis, the authors commend a humble, contingent (as it relies on the continual renewing power of God's Spirit), contextual, and Christ-centered approach to the enduring challenges of culture and relationships. This book is a gift I wish upon every person and team that serves in contexts of cultural difference."

—**Christopher L. Flanders**, Abilene Christian University

"This book is for ministry leaders who desire to live out Jesus's words, 'By this everyone will know that you are my disciples, if you love one another.' As an expression of love, Lingenfelter has opened the door and held it wide open to allow us to learn from a diverse group of ministry leaders. This nuanced work will challenge our assumptions about what it means to pick up our cross as we shepherd multinational teams. Please read it, but don't read it all at once—read it, pray it, live it, and read it again . . . so that the world may know that we are truly his disciples."

—**Hyon Kim**, SIM International

# Teamwork
# Cross-Culturally

# Teamwork Cross-Culturally

## CHRIST-CENTERED SOLUTIONS FOR LEADING MULTINATIONAL TEAMS

SHERWOOD G. LINGENFELTER

AND JULIE A. GREEN

**Baker Academic**

*a division of Baker Publishing Group*
Grand Rapids, Michigan

© 2022 by Sherwood G. Lingenfelter

Published by Baker Academic
a division of Baker Publishing Group
PO Box 6287, Grand Rapids, MI 49516-6287
www.bakeracademic.com

Printed in the United States of America

Library of Congress Cataloging-in-Publication Data
Names: Lingenfelter, Sherwood G., author. | Green, Julie A., author.
Title: Teamwork cross-culturally : Christ-centered solutions for leading multinational teams / Sherwood G. Lingenfelter and Julie A. Green.
Description: Grand Rapids, Michigan : Baker Academic, a division of Baker Publishing Group, [2022] | Includes bibliographical references and index.
Identifiers: LCCN 2021049564 | ISBN 9781540965448 (paperback) | ISBN 9781540965639 (casebound) | ISBN 9781493436736 (ebook) | ISBN 9781493436743 (pdf)
Subjects: LCSH: Missions—Theory. | Christian leadership. | Christianity and culture. | Multinational work teams.
Classification: LCC BV2063 .L4355 2022 | DDC 266—dc23/eng/20211103
LC record available at https://lccn.loc.gov/2021049564

Baker Publishing Group publications use paper produced from sustainable forestry practices and post-consumer waste whenever possible.

22   23   24   25   26   27   28        7   6   5   4   3   2   1

To Julie Green, who imagined this book and dedicated four years of her life to thinking through the "wicked problems and clumsy solutions" of multinational teamwork. She went to be with her Lord in the prime of her life, October 11, 2020. We celebrate her life and legacy by completing this work.

# Contents

# Abbreviations

GPM    Global Pentecostal Mission (pseudonym)
PILAT  Pacific Institute of Languages, Arts and Translation
PNG    Papua New Guinea
SAT    Southeast Asia Team (a branch of SIL International)
SIL    SIL International (partner of national Wycliffe organizations)
SIM    SIM International (global church planting mission)

# Preface

This book is the fourth book in a series that addresses the issues of culture and the practice of cross-cultural ministry. The first, *Ministering Cross-Culturally*, was written for people called to serve and witness for Jesus Christ in any culture other than their own. Developing a framework of contrasting values, the book guides readers to begin by understanding their values as culture-bearing people, then to understand the contrasting values of others, and ultimately to learn how to add to their cultural repertoire to be effective in cross-cultural ministry.

The second book, *Teaching Cross-Culturally*, was written by my wife, Judith, and me for the Western-trained educator who is working or planning to work in a non-Western educational setting or in the multicultural schools and universities in the major cities of North America. The goal of this work is to help teachers understand their personal culture of teaching and learning and to equip them to become effective learners in another cultural context, with a specific focus on learning for teaching.

The third book, *Leading Cross-Culturally*, speaks to Western and non-Western leaders who are working with or planning to work with and lead people in multicultural teams and ministry contexts. It gives significant attention to issues of cultural diversity and ministry partnerships that cross cultural boundaries and to the way that cultural bias of every kind creates obstacles to effective leadership and ministry partnerships.

The intended audience for this book, *Teamwork Cross-Culturally*, includes leaders and team members who have accepted the challenges of twenty-first-century "mission with"—rather than "mission to"— members of the body of Christ within the global church. The practice of "mission to" often fostered patterns of cultural domination and distortion of the gospel. In his work *The Next Christendom*, Philip Jenkins describes the radical shift in the momentum of the global church from Europe and North America to the Southern Hemisphere, so that by the end of the twentieth century, Christians in Africa, Latin America, and Asia far outnumbered those in Europe and North America. This global expansion of the church has also led to a radical change in mission: mission is now understood to be from everywhere to everywhere. Thus "mission with" is an appropriate response of the global church. But once again, because of the vast diversity in cultures and nations around the globe, "mission with" is much more challenging than the twentieth-century practice of "mission to" peoples without Christ.

A book of this length cannot address all or even most of the substantive issues that teams encounter when their members come together from very diverse national and cultural backgrounds to work together for the "mission of God." We acknowledge the exceptional contributions that Evelyn and Richard Hibbert, Sheryl Takagi Silzer, and Johan Linder have made to this topic.[1] We also recommend that readers consult other works on leadership and culture that we cannot cover here. This book is not a primer on how to manage multinational team dynamics. Further, we do not offer "solutions" or a "curriculum" to find solutions here. Rather, our contributing authors illustrate how unique leaders engage uniquely formed multinational teams and address complex, real-world problems in order to find their own distinctive pathways "in Christ." Their stories show how each leader discovers what the world would call "clumsy" ways forward in their commitment to work together for the mission of God.

---

1. Hibbert and Hibbert, *Leading Multicultural Teams*; Silzer, *Biblical Multicultural Teams*; and Linder, *Working in Multicultural Teams*.

This book then brings together the challenge of "wicked problems" in cross-cultural teamwork and substantive case studies of "in-Christ" solutions to those problems. The book's authors and contributors are grateful to God, who "has rescued us from the dominion of darkness [the origin of wicked problems] and brought us into the kingdom of the Son he loves" (Col. 1:13). Therefore, in response to our gratitude we have several goals for this book. The first goal is to help leaders and team members understand the nature of wicked problems and the inadequacy of common sense, routine cultural learning, past experience, and normal team dialogue and leadership to resolve such problems. Wicked problems are never "solved"—they resist management solutions, and that is why scholars call them "wicked." At best, effective leaders and "soft power" may cobble together temporary "clumsy" solutions that ameliorate internal conflict until the next crisis.

The second goal is to guide readers to biblical essentials that are foundational for leaders and team members who are from radically diverse backgrounds but seek to engage in teamwork cross-culturally "in Christ." You may wonder whether the twenty-first century is so different culturally that the Scriptures do not speak to these issues, but I (Sherwood) would like to convince you that Paul, called by Jesus to proclaim his name to the gentiles, was the first missionary to confront this "wicked" spiritual and cultural blindness problem in ministry. By examining the cultural and interpersonal conflicts in Paul's Letters, I hope to show you how Paul experienced deep frustration and even anger about such conflict and—led by the Holy Spirit—discovered the spiritual power and pathway to engage and frame "clumsy" but Christ-filled solutions to such problems.

The third goal of this book is to equip readers to discern and respond "in Christ" to six areas of "in the world" deceptions that challenge leaders and team members. Three of these areas are organizational: management, problem solving, and return on investment. Three are interpersonal: values conflicts, personality needs or hungers, and spiritual self-deception. The five case studies included in this book illustrate how the ordinary details of social and cultural life and the secret and deceptive ways of our spiritual enemy—Satan—may deceive us and actually destroy the unity in Christ that God desires for us. These case studies reveal the actual practice of multinational teamwork in diverse ministry contexts, allowing us to examine and compare the situations to uncover the issues in play and understand how leaders and team members have sought to stand against the forces for evil.

The fourth goal is to provide readers with practical, twenty-first-century case studies that answer the question: What kind of leadership and sacrifice will serve teams to enable them to bring the gospel to the nations today? The contributing authors tell their stories of how they have applied Paul's teaching to equip and mobilize global Christians for God's mission today. Each of these authors has reflected on his or her personal journey of leadership through the lens of Scripture, applying the biblical metaphors of leadership—shepherd, servant, steward—from the four Gospels, and the ministry triad of the work of faith, the labor of love, and steadfast hope from the Pauline Epistles. We believe that these chapters provide real-life examples that readers can use to examine their own ministry practices, and from these cases find applications to test and create in-Christ solutions for their unique and personal situations of cross-cultural teamwork.

I am indebted to many colleagues and friends who read earlier drafts of this work and gave me substantive and constructive feedback. Peter Lin, Hyon Kim, and David Bremner gave generously of their time, and their critical insights and helpful suggestions made the second draft of this work far superior to the first. I am also grateful for other reviewers—Lorraine Dierck, Anita Koeshall, Betsy Glanville, Dick Brogden, and Sharon Mertz—who encouraged me in the manuscript review process. I am especially grateful to the contributing authors—Penny Bakewell, Robert and Elizabeth McLean (pseudonyms), Matthew Crosland, and Martins Atanda—who walked with me in a six-month process of drafts, revisions, editing, and review that has led to this completed work. My beloved wife, Judith, prayed with me daily, read every draft chapter, discussed new insights on our morning walks, and rejoiced with me each step of the way. My pastor son, Joel, read the final draft of the manuscript, challenging and encouraging me and contributing invaluable insights as an objective first-time reader of this work.

I am deeply indebted to Julie Green, my coauthor, who was the driving force behind this book and whose work illuminated for me the high risk of wicked problems for global mission. Julie studied with both Judith and me at Biola University for her BA and MA degrees. We partnered with Julie in Thailand for SIL workshops and dialogue about the challenges she experienced in teamwork, and she kept in touch with us personally and intellectually over thirty-five years of ministry in South Asia. After she completed her PhD with me at Fuller Theological Seminary, I borrowed her sensitive insights and rigorous analysis to encourage others ministering in multinational teams. When her battle with cancer ended her life in 2020, it was my joy to complete this work for God's people called to "mission with" in the next decade.

# 1

What Are Wicked Problems
and In-Christ Solutions?

SHERWOOD G. LINGENFELTER
AND JULIE A. GREEN

## Starting Language Programs in Asia: A Case Study

One of my (Julie's) first assignments as leader of a multinational team was to help my team start language development programs—alphabet, grammar, dictionary, stories—that would lead to translation of Scripture. My organization, Southeast Asia Team (SAT), was a new branch of our sponsoring organization, SIL International.[1] We hoped to recruit more workers, so preparing a program plan was essential in order to apply for new visas—a challenging task in our national context. We turned to SIL leaders who had experience and expertise to help us to prepare our language development proposal. As a result of my past experience and success in starting language development

1. SIL International is the global organization to which organizations associated with Wycliffe Bible Translators send members to support language development and Bible translation ministries.

projects in another South Asian context, I was quite confident that I knew what we needed to make this current work come together.

My first task was to get to know each of my team members in SAT, who were also members of SIL. As I looked around in our first meeting together, I saw godly men and women from Indonesia, Denmark, the Philippines, the United Kingdom, Australia, and the United States struggling with our assignment. I was concerned, so I asked them about the difficulties they had encountered while starting new language development projects within SIL, and they quickly told me stories of their troubles. They asserted that SIL staff did not write language development work into project proposals—or, when they did, the goals and time frames were utterly inappropriate. They also complained that when SIL staff had written language projects, they had not allowed local communities to have any say or ownership. Additionally, my team members wanted the local church to be involved in the work from the beginning, even if it slowed down the progress of the project.

After talking with my team, I relayed what I had learned to SIL leaders. They also affirmed that language development work must happen from within the existing church structures and with other national nongovernmental organizations. They went on to explain that they did not want to duplicate work or do anything on their own. They also assured me that future project proposals could have room in them for research and development and local involvement. I was reassured by their response, and—believing that our goals were similar—I quickly outlined a strategic framework that would allow the language development team to start projects locally while at the same time considering SIL's (our sponsoring partner) concerns.

When I presented the language development framework to the leaders in SIL, they were very supportive, and at the next board meeting, they approved the strategic framework document. They also encouraged me to work with the language development team to reach out to local churches and organizations to create proposals that would work for language development projects.

Thinking that I had bridged the organizational gap between my team members and our SIL partners, I called a meeting of SAT language development workers. The agenda was to discuss how we would do language development projects within the organizational framework I had outlined to SIL. I anticipated that this framework would help us focus our planning and give us the freedom we sought. I sent the agenda of our meeting and the proposed framework to these field teams.

I was enormously proud of the work I had done negotiating and then writing the strategic framework document. It did not take long, however, for my pride to deflate to dismay and then quickly to annoyance as complaining and condemning emails began to invade my inbox. In this flood of emails, each field team of SAT took turns complaining about the strategy and tearing it down.

In short, my team was angry with me and resisted everything I proposed. They rejected the way I had processed this decision and dismissed my proposal since it failed to achieve the organizational revolt against SIL that so many of them desired. I thought my recommendation for collaboration, defining common goals, and focusing on strategy between SAT and SIL personnel seemed quite reasonable. I sought a mutual path forward by limiting the discussion to ways we could cooperate positively and refused to entertain exit strategies that were outside my leadership mandate. Unfortunately, my attempts to lead only created more conflicts and polarization within the team and caused more damage to our relationships.

As I cried to the Lord and then reflected on the polarizing positions of my teammates, I knew there was no right answer about how to make decisions on this team. I had run into a sticky, wicked problem without understanding it, and my desire to use what I thought was my authority to control the process and create certainty was making it worse.

## Why Name It a "Wicked Problem"?

First of all, no one involved in this case would permit Julie to call this a "wicked problem." "We are good people; we just disagree on the fundamentals of how to go about language development. Yes, the

situation is complex, and yes, we have different experiences, but . . . I
am right and the rest of the team just doesn't get it! I pray that they
will wake up to the reality we are facing in these tribal languages. I
can see it clearly—why don't they see it, and why doesn't Julie agree
with me?"

The essence of a "wicked problem," as opposed to a critical problem (such as a fire) or a routine problem (such as a budget), is that
both the problem and the solution are fundamentally inscrutable—
neither can be completely understood or clearly explained because of
their complexities. As Julie describes in her case study, the conflicting
values of her teammates and their objections to the process that she
or others proposed were so polarized that the group members rejected
every "management" solution offered. Julie was confident she had
crafted a compromise pathway that would satisfy most involved, but
her teammates did not agree, and—as we will see later—the uncertainty about the problem increased the harder she tried to manage it.

Julie recognized the deep challenge of polarization within her
teammates. In their conversations, they mentally framed one another's
positions as "either-or" choices. They debated with one another about
the strengths and weaknesses of "my" position as opposed to "your"
or "their" position. They exercised patterns learned in their years
of education—there is a single right answer to the problem—and
each was confident about what that answer was. Out of their diverse
personal and cultural backgrounds, they were deeply suspicious of
approaches they had not experienced. If Julie had been trained in
the business practices of "polarity management,"[2] she may have had
better luck with her colleagues, but many other factors were at work
in their respective backgrounds.

These team members had all experienced a calling to the mission
of Bible translation, raised personal financial support, and sacrificed
much in their home settings—Indonesia, Denmark, the Philippines,
the United Kingdom, Australia, the United States—to make the journey to Southeast Asia. Their churches and supporters back home had
high expectations for them, and they also had high expectations for

2. Johnson, *Polarity Management*.

themselves. They did not feel accountable to SAT, and even less to SIL. They did not owe allegiance to SAT or SIL, nor had they developed the kind of loyalty Julie had because of her years of experience with SIL. They had been trained differently in their respective home countries, studying common topics but mentored by people who understood these topics from different perspectives. As relatively new members of Julie's team, they acted more as independent contractors than as members of a team. Some saw no need even to be a team, believing their role was one that could be performed alone.

As people engaging across cultures, our problems are manifold. First of all, we know only what we know—the childhood and adult experiences of language, culture, and faith that have shaped us as persons. Within these limitations, we are inherently afraid of what we do not know and of the risk of losing what we do know and what we turn to for comfort and security.

Further, as human beings we have a host of cravings that drive us daily—thirst; hunger for food, shelter, comfort, and intimacy; and sleep—and emotional needs such as the needs for love, security, acceptance, meaning, significance, authority, and control. James reminds us that "each person is tempted when they are dragged away by their own evil desire and enticed. Then, after desire has conceived, it gives birth to sin; and sin, when it is full-grown, gives birth to death" (James 1:14–15).

Finally, the Scriptures teach us that we have an enemy, the devil, who is always working to discredit God and deceive us. Later in this work we will reflect on the hungers or evil desires that often deceive us as persons and the deceptions that the devil uses to deceive the body of Christ. He is the ruler of darkness, and Christ alone—the Lamb that was slain—is able to deliver us from that darkness.

This chapter will conclude this discussion of Julie's wicked problem by considering three additional questions. Given the difficulties of wicked problems, (1) Is "mission with" an option for sharing the gospel? (2) How do we respond to such fragmentation and division in the body of Christ when we are called for God's mission? (3) How can we, in such situations of cultural complexity, ever find unity in Christ?

## Is "Mission with" Optional in Christ?

Given the challenges and difficulties Julie experienced in her case study, is "mission with" optional? Many churches and mission organizations have made the decision to stay within their own national and denominational cultures and to send missionaries out to unreached peoples and plant churches of "our kind" in other nations. Lorraine Dierck, a mission leader observing missionaries who have given up on "mission with" teams in Thailand, comments:

> The complexity of cross-cultural communication continues to baffle and confuse people engaged in the task of frontier missions. A young missionary to Thailand said, "I came to Thailand with a big vision, and with a lot of skill and enthusiasm. I know I have a lot to contribute to this ministry. But the Thai leaders go ahead and do whatever they want without discussing anything with me. I feel totally useless. I'm planning to go back to England as soon as possible."[3]

Many, like this young man, have reverted to the old colonial option—mission within my own sphere of power and influence. They have found this far easier to manage, and they plant churches in the denominational patterns and divisions they have experienced at home. But is this route—which is clearly easier to manage—the purpose and intent of God?

Julie and I began this work with a proposition that "mission with" is the only feasible paradigm[4] to fulfill the purpose of God in the twenty-first century. Given that her teammates in practice did not agree, we asked ourselves, How do we know that "mission with" is God's purpose for our time?

As we reflected on this question, we read from John 17: "I have given them the glory that you gave me, that they may be one as we are one—I in them and you in me—so that they may be brought to complete unity. Then the world will know that you sent me and have loved them even as you have loved me" (vv. 22–23). The intent in this prayer is clear: "complete unity" is how the world will know Christ

3. Dierck, "Leadership and Patron-Client Structures," 106.
4. Bazzell, "Who Is Our Cornelius?," 110.

and God's love through Christ. As we read further in Scripture, we saw how the apostle Paul also called local believers in Ephesus to this same end: "Make every effort to keep the unity of the Spirit through the bond of peace. There is one body and one Spirit, just as you were called to one hope when you were called; one Lord, one faith, one baptism; one God and Father of all, who is over all and through all and in all" (Eph. 4:3–6). While Paul's reflection on the church as "one body" was far smaller in scale than the reality we understand today, the implications for mission are the same. In our current global context, we have the same resources to be one as did first-century Christians. However, unity is possible only if we together are willing to suffer with Christ as we engage in "mission with" for the sake of the gospel.

## Mission from a Position of Weakness[5]

So how can we respond to the reality of fragmentation and division in the body of Christ? Paul Jeong, in his doctoral research on Korean missions, notes how the apostle Paul was grounded in the reality of "Christ crucified" and defined his mission to the gentiles in terms of the "weakness of the cross." In his letters to the Corinthians, Paul declares, "We preach Christ crucified: a stumbling block to Jews and *foolishness* to Gentiles" (1 Cor. 1:23); "I came to you in *weakness* with great fear and trembling" (2:3); "If I must boast, I will boast of the things that show my *weakness*" (2 Cor. 11:30). Jeong challenges us to reflect deeply on Paul's emphasis on mission out of a position of weakness.[6] As Christ was crucified on the cross, "he was crucified in *weakness*, yet he lives by God's power. Likewise, we are weak in him, yet by God's power we will live with him in our dealing with you" (13:4). Mission from a position of weakness, then, is not the absence of power but rather complete reliance on the power of God.

By participating in the cross of Christ, the community is "being transformed into the image of Christ."[7] What does this mean for the

5. This section draws on Newbigin, *Open Secret*, 5.
6. Jeong, "Essence of Leadership," 127–28.
7. Thompson, *Apostle of Persuasion*, 167.

practice of "mission with" leadership and teamwork? Fundamentally, it means that we must reject every form of domination in leadership. In the chapters that follow, we will examine how people usually use one of three forms of control—hierarchy, group, or individual control. Each form uses domination of others to achieve control:

- The leaders on top of a hierarchy dominate the subjects below.
- The group subjugates all its members, forcing conformity to the group will.
- The individual does what is "right in his own eyes" irrespective of others.

Julie's team members were all concerned about controlling their language development projects, but they each envisioned different options to achieve that control. Domination/subjugation is always a work of the enemy, who seeks to undermine and destroy the household of faith and the functional body of Christ.

How do we respond to our cultural bondage and the "wicked problems" that result when we insist on our own way? The only truly effective way is "in Christ." John the Baptist was the first to point out the way: "Look, the Lamb of God, who takes away the sin of the world!" (John 1:29). John is calling us not just to look at Jesus but to encounter, hold, and be held by the Savior who takes away the sins of the world. In the chapters that follow, we will repeatedly look to Jesus, asking what it means to be a team and to do teamwork "in Christ." Our motivation and method must be wholly anchored in Jesus: he is our only hope to overcome "in the world" wicked problems.

## Unity in Christ—Teamwork

Multinational teamwork can be either a validation of the history of the church—fractured, hostile in its factions, and riven with congregational and denominational disunity—or a missional expression of the body of Christ, reconciled as "one body to God by the cross," characterized by "the good news of peace," and belonging "to God's household," being "a place where God lives through the Spirit" (Eph. 2:16–22 CEB). Mission scholar Pablo Deiros argues that disunity is the norm for church and mission because we have lost focus on the "meaning of the church as the body of Christ and especially as the bride of Christ."[8]

In the chapters that follow, we give concrete examples of what it means for multinational teams to be local expressions of the body of Christ on mission. We will see in each the kinds of conflict and polarization that Julie reported in her case study, and we will see how leaders responded "in Christ." Building on our mutual understanding that Christ died to break down the wall of hostility between Jews and the *ethne* (gentiles) of the world (Eph. 2:14), these leaders worked to establish peace among team members by focusing on the individuals' new identity in Christ as one people of God. Further, "God's purpose is now to show the rulers and powers in the heavens the many different varieties of his wisdom through the church" (3:10 CEB). Of particular note here is God's demonstration of "many different varieties of his wisdom"—illustrated in Julie's case study and in the case studies provided by the contributing authors in part 3 of this book.

In addition, we will explore the important message of Christ reported in John 17—unity! As I have written elsewhere,[9] this unity is not uniformity but rather a unity of purpose. It is a commitment to a common mission in which every part of the body esteems the other parts and every part does its work. In the following case studies, we spell out how believers can achieve this kind of unity in the context of radical cultural diversity. We show how multinational team members can understand and work through the challenges of wicked problems in their teamwork by making this kind of unity a common goal.

Deiros conceptualizes this kind of mission as a mission from the perspective of the future, a mission that anticipates the return of Christ for his bride. Thus, we prepare ourselves as that bride by living and serving out of our identity, with love for him. This picture

8. Deiros, "Eschatology and Mission," 274.
9. Lingenfelter, *Leadership in the Way of the Cross*, 106–7.

seeks to capture the idea that Christ is the center of mission from everywhere to everywhere—"He is in touch with all the nations and all the nations are drawn to Him."[10]

Finally, Evelyne Reisacher, who was professor of Islamic studies at Fuller Theological Seminary, reminded us that the power and the mission that Jesus gave to the church are about the joy we experience when we become part of God's mission through Jesus to reconcile the world to himself.[11] When we are willing to suffer with Christ and serve as members of his body in unity, the outcome will be an overwhelming joy: "Dear friends, don't be surprised about the fiery trials that have come among you to test you. . . . Instead, rejoice as you share Christ's suffering . . . so that you may also have overwhelming joy when his glory is revealed" (1 Pet. 4:12–13 CEB).

10. Deiros, "Eschatology and Mission," 279.
11. Reisacher, *Joyful Witness*, 16–17.

# PART 1

# Biblical Foundations for In-Christ Responses

Given that "mission with" is necessary in the twenty-first century and that wicked problems are endemic to forming multinational teams, what Christ-centered solutions do we find in Scripture for leading such teams? Our first challenge is to ask, Do we see any precedent for "mission with" and wicked problems in New Testament texts? If so, how do New Testament writers persuade and guide twenty-first-century multinational teams to work together in unity?

We are convinced that Scripture speaks to both of these issues. We found fruitful evidence of a first-century wicked problem in the book of Galatians, and I discovered in A. Sue Russell's book *In the World but Not of the World* concrete evidence of how early church leaders engaged the challenges of "in the world" thinking to live out the gospel in a hostile Roman Empire. James Thompson, in his book *Apostle of Persuasion*, provided me with a clear exposition of how the apostle Paul sought to persuade gentile converts to live transformed lives and be united in Christ.

The goal of part 1 is to guide readers to biblical essentials that are foundational for leaders and team members who are from radically diverse backgrounds but seek to engage in cross-cultural teamwork in Christ. Chapter 2 presents an analysis of Paul's wicked problem with the circumcision faction from Jerusalem that followed him everywhere he preached, dividing the unity of his team and seeking to make new Christian converts into Jews. Chapter 3 examines what it means to be centered "in Christ" and to embrace Paul's triad of the work of faith, the labor of love, and steadfast hope as a framework from which to lead multinational teams for "mission with."

# 2

IIIIIIIIIIIIIIIIIIIIIIIIIIIIIIIIIIIIIIIIIIIIIIIIIIIIIIIIIIIIIIIIIIIIIIIIIIIIIIIIIIIIIIIIIIIIIIIIIIIIIIIIIIIIIIIIIIIIIIIIIIIIIII

# Paul's Wicked Problem
# and In-Christ Defense

SHERWOOD G. LINGENFELTER

## Confrontation in Jerusalem and Antioch: A Case Study

Then after fourteen years I went up to Jerusalem again with Barnabas, and I took Titus along also. I went there because of a revelation, and I laid out the gospel that I preach to the Gentiles for them. But I did it privately with the influential leaders to make sure that I wouldn't be working or that I hadn't worked for nothing. However, not even Titus, who was with me and who was a Greek, was required to be circumcised. But false brothers and sisters, who were brought in secretly, slipped in to spy on our freedom, which we have in Christ Jesus, and to make us slaves. We didn't give in and submit to them for a single moment, so that the truth of the gospel would continue to be with you. (Gal. 2:1–5 CEB)

But when Cephas [Peter] came to Antioch, I opposed him to his face, because he was wrong. He had been eating with the Gentiles before certain people came from James. But when they came, he began to back out and separate himself, because he was afraid of the people

13

who promoted circumcision. And the rest of the Jews also joined him in this hypocrisy so that even Barnabas got carried away with them in their hypocrisy. But when I saw that they weren't acting consistently with the truth of the gospel, I said to Cephas in front of everyone, "If you, though you're a Jew, live like a Gentile and not like a Jew, how can you require the Gentiles to live like Jews?" (Gal. 2:11–14 CEB)

## What Makes This Case a Wicked Problem?

Cross-cultural teamwork problems are not peculiar to the twenty-first century. The apostle Paul faced these issues in the first century as God's chosen messenger to the gentiles. Jewish and gentile relationships were at best filled with suspicion, and they often degenerated into hostility and even violence. In Luke's account of Paul and Barnabas's first missionary journey, their encounters are fraught with both spiritual and cultural conflict. When Paul invited Timothy and Titus to be ministry partners, he was welcoming uncircumcised, Greek-speaking believers to become his right-hand partners in ministry. This decision was positive for Paul's cross-cultural evangelistic ministry in gentile cities, but for his Jewish-Christian colleagues in Jerusalem and Antioch, it created a problem that turned out to be a continuous threat to Paul's ministry everywhere.

Paul, from the beginning, was an outsider to the Jewish-Christian movement and had no personal contact with the leaders or the fellowship in Jerusalem. The reality was that this separation was mutual—these Jerusalem believers did not trust Saul/Paul, and they did not welcome him into their company (Gal. 1:17–24). So in Jerusalem he named the opposition "false brothers and sisters . . . [who] slipped in to spy on our freedom." The circumcision faction—"false brothers and sisters," deceptive enemies of the gospel—was adamant about maintaining the purity of the Christian community regarding the law. To eat with gentiles, they maintained, was to pollute the community and defile those who were obedient to the law. Paul's position was as strong as their opposition: "We didn't give in and submit to them for a single moment, so that the truth of the gospel would continue to be with you [Galatians]" (2:4–5 CEB).

Paul asserts his innocence regarding the laws of purity and pollution on the basis of his understanding of the freedom in Christ that comes in the gospel, and he defends his position and actions, noting that the "influential leaders" have supported his understanding of the gospel and his preaching to uncircumcised gentiles. For further validation, he notes that "James, Cephas, and John, who are considered to be key leaders, shook hands with me and Barnabas as equals when they recognized the grace that was given to me" (Gal. 2:9 CEB). But Paul was stunned when these fellow Christian leaders—Cephas (Peter) and even Barnabas—betrayed him in Antioch. As members of the Jerusalem establishment, they feared the collective pressure of the circumcision faction among the believers in Judea. Privately these leaders had supported Paul in Antioch, but when members of the Jerusalem faction arrived, Peter and even Barnabas publicly submitted to the pressure of their shared culture. Paul's statement, "I opposed him to his face, because he was wrong" (v. 11), highlights the moral dimension of the leaders' choice. For Paul, this was false behavior, denying the gospel of Jesus Christ.

### Fear—the Root of "Wicked" Problems

What was the source of Peter's fear of these "certain people" promoting circumcision?

First, Paul accuses Peter and Barnabas of hypocrisy: their actions suggest a fear of losing face—they did not want to be seen eating with gentile believers. But for Peter, the matter is perhaps a deeper fear for personal safety. If we remember his story (Acts 12), Peter fled from Jerusalem after Herod executed the apostle James and imprisoned Peter for execution. Herod planned this because it pleased the priests and the Sanhedrin, who ruled by power and fear, exercising both as often as they felt was necessary to accomplish their objectives. So Peter was already living under a cloud of suspicion. The members of the circumcision faction not only were adamant about purity and pollution; they also wanted to keep in favor with the ruling priestly class and the Sanhedrin.

Peter's fears and those of James, John, and Barnabas stemmed from very legitimate threats to their lives and their respectability and honor in the community. Herod and the Jews of the Sanhedrin had the power to kill. Christ-followers such as James and Stephen had already lost their lives. And Paul, with his rejection of circumcision and insistence on table fellowship with gentiles, was threatening their acceptance as leaders among the Jewish converts in Jerusalem. As with all human beings, their way of life—their authority as leaders, collective community, and strong moral inclination to honor the "law" of the community—predisposed them toward specific actions to mediate and, if possible, to control, reduce, or remove risk from their lives.

## Paul's Rebuke of "Wicked Problem" Behaviors

Given the challenges of false brothers and weak gentile converts, Paul's most powerful insight occurs in his question to his gentile readers: "After knowing God, . . . how can you turn back again to the weak and worthless world system?" (Gal. 4:9 CEB). This question is Paul's judgment on all ways of life apart from Christ. They are all weak and worthless, enslaving humans to a particular way of life apart from God. This is precisely the issue that we will deal with in part 2 of this book. All of us are in bondage to the way of life given to us by our loving parents and by our communities of origin. Our past experiences and ways of life enslave us, and—no matter how hard we try—our identities, our thought patterns, our habits of life, and our assessments of others apart from Christ are weak and worthless. The antidote to this enslavement is knowing and being known by God through Jesus Christ, but for the Galatians and perhaps for us, this is not enough.

Lest we declare that we are above such human foibles, think about the other characters in Paul's story. Peter followed Jesus during Jesus's entire earthly ministry. He was the one called by the Lord to be the apostle to the circumcised. He preached in power on the day of Pentecost and in the following decade. At the Jerusalem Council, he concurred with Paul on the question of freedom in Christ, and

he shared table fellowship with Titus until members of the circumcision faction arrived in Antioch from Jerusalem. At that moment
in Antioch, Peter defaulted to his former way of life, giving up his
freedom for the sake of retaining his honor among the circumcised.
But even more astonishing is the fact that Barnabas, Paul's missionary
companion and advocate for many years, also defaulted under this
pressure, abandoning his fellow servants, Titus and Paul, to keep his
honor among these visiting Jews from Jerusalem. Why would these
distinguished servants of Jesus Christ be so weak in the face of this
opposition? We must never underestimate the power of habits of life
that have been with us for a long time.

In my book *Transforming Culture*, I (Sherwood) argue that one's
culture or way of life is both palace and prison to its members.[1] Paul
suggests that "God has imprisoned all human beings in their own
disobedience only to show mercy to them all" (Rom. 11:32 NJB).
Further, in his Letter to the Galatians (3:1–13), he warns that "all who
rely on the works of the law are under a curse" (v. 10). This includes
not only the Jewish law but also the gentile ways of life (Eph. 4).

Despite that enslavement and curse, culture is a "palace" in the
sense that we cannot live apart from it. We cannot receive a gospel
that does not speak into our language and way of life. But the glory
of the gospel is this: God, in his mercy, sets us free from both the
enslavement of any system of law (Rom. 2) and the curse of our ways
of life through the death and resurrection of Jesus Christ. And, by
the work of the Holy Spirit, we may experience the renewing of our
minds in Christ Jesus, which enables us to be servants of Christ to
the people around us who do not know him.

## Teamwork "in the World" or "in Christ"?

So what does this story mean for our reflection on and analysis of
crises and conflict in contemporary multinational teams? First and
foremost, we all are sociocultural beings, and—like the people in
this story—we live in the world where our default pattern is to seek

1. Lingenfelter, *Transforming Culture*, 19–20.

security in and through our cultural and moral choices. This tendency is particularly strong in situations of tension and uncertainty when people who hold different views enter the room and challenge our understanding or decisions. Paul reminds us that our natural state is slavery to a way of life that limits our choices by fears, habits, and bondage to a "weak and worthless world system."

As we reflect on crises and conflict in contemporary multinational teams, it is helpful to analyze the diversity of thinking among the participants in Paul's story regarding their "in the world" perceptions of threat and the management of risk. The patterns we see in the Galatian crisis may be summarized as follows:

1. Theological self-justification: the Jewish-Christian faction

   These Christians could not separate their faith in Christ from their identity as Jews and their habits of separation from and even hostility toward gentiles. If gentiles believed in Jesus, that was good, but to have fellowship with "us," these "outsiders" *had to become insiders*—which meant circumcision (for males) and conformity to the legal requirements (eating, feast days, and other regulations) of Jerusalem Judaism. *Justifying themselves theologically* by arguing that Paul's dissenting view was against Moses, was unacceptable, and must be stopped, they crusaded against Paul, following him wherever he went, *seeking to reconvert* gentiles to the Jewish-Christian theological position and their view of the *theologically correct way* of following Jesus. Paul clearly identifies them as "false brothers," not following the way of Christ but giving in to the deceiver, who always undermines God's message to humanity.

2. Internal conflict, self-protection: the mission team

   James, Peter, Barnabas, Timothy, and Titus—mission directors and partners—lived in the tension of their historic Jewish and gentile commitments and their new lives in Christ. Their emotional responses and behaviors reflect that *internal conflict*. When these leaders visited Antioch, a gentile community, they had freedom to engage with Titus and the gentile believers, teaching them, praying with them, and enjoying table fellowship with them apart from the Mosaic way. However, when members of the "Jerusalem faction" arrived, James, Peter, and Barnabas rejected Titus and the others and separated themselves *to protect their "in the world" status and honor* in Jerusalem. In essence, they conformed to the pressure of their Jewish heritage and were conflicted—spiritually and socially—in their responses.

3. Fearing risk, grasping for control and assurance: the Galatians
Paul comprehended a radical change concerning what it means to be "in Christ." New believers became members of a new community in which the identity of being in Christ "transcended ethnic, status, economic and gender differences in the way that marked not only membership in the community but also defined the way they were to interact with one another."[2] For Paul, there was no risk in leaving his Jewish status, customs, rules of good behavior, and worship behind—and further, doing so was essential to the mission of preaching the gospel.

The new Galatian converts, on the other hand, had yet to comprehend the essence of what it means to be "in Christ," so they were *readily deceived* when the Jerusalem faction sought to convince them—through the ancient texts of Moses—that a new set of "in the world" rules was essential to their newfound faith. As the ancient serpent said to Eve, "God didn't really mean that you would die," the Jerusalem faction said to the gentiles, "You must follow our rules, festivals, and structures to be set apart for God." These converts had already taken a *great risk* in their conversion, which separated them from their previous status as "in the world," so a new set of rules, grounded in the authority of ancient texts, apparently provided self-control and moral structure[3] that gave them assurance. Paul had to draw from those same texts, citing the stories of Abraham and Sarah (Gal. 3), to convince them otherwise.

2. Russell, *In the World but Not of the World*, 146–47.
3. Thompson, *Apostle of Persuasion*, 172.

## Paul's In-Christ Defense

> For all of you who were baptized into Christ have clothed yourselves
> with Christ. There is neither Jew nor Gentile, neither slave nor free,
> nor is there male and female, for you are all one in Christ Jesus. (Gal.
> 3:27–28)

Our power to change and serve effectively together is grounded
only and fully in Jesus Christ. We have received the Spirit of Christ
through faith. We live and work in the power of the Spirit alone, not by
any system of human rules or works that we can devise. Further, Paul
marks a substantive change of identity for us all: our social identity
in the world no longer matters within the Christian community—we
are "all one in Christ Jesus."

Finally, Paul declares to the Galatians and us that the systems of
rules and laws that we devise to control offenses and to ensure social
power, honor, purity, and innocence are utterly inadequate. These
rules and regulations not only fail to achieve their intended ends but
also enslave the people who follow them. But in Christ, everything is
changed! "Christ has set us free for freedom. Therefore, stand firm
and don't submit to the bondage of slavery again" (Gal. 5:1 CEB).

The application of Paul's in-Christ defense for cross-cultural
teamwork is profound. All members of a team bring with them the
systems of rules, values, and expectations that were devised by their
parents and ancestors to control offenses and to ensure social power,
honor, purity, and innocence. In times of crisis, our enemy the deceiver leads us to default to our preconversion systems of thinking,
feeling, and action. These are systems that Paul says enslave us. Even
if we have the courage to reject our culture of origin, we often easily
adopt a new system, as the Galatians did, to assure ourselves that we
have self-control and moral structure. In our relationships with one
another, we then do battle to defend our way of life. Paul shouts to
Peter, James, Barnabas, Timothy, Titus, the Jerusalem faction, and
the Galatians, "Christ has set us free for freedom. . . . Don't submit
to the bondage of slavery again"!

## REFLECTION QUESTIONS

- Why is it hard for us to imagine that our customs and habits of life could be an obstacle to effective teamwork and to our witness of the gospel?

- What is the difference between how your culture defines your social position in the world and how your social position may be redefined in Christ?

- Can you identify the last time you justified yourself theologically? Or the last time you felt the need to protect yourself in a situation when others pressured you? Or the last time fear drove you to seek control of a situation?

- Can you name two or three situations in your life experience when you did battle to defend your way of life? How do these situations make you feel about Paul's shout?

# 3

||||||||||||||||||||||||||||||||||||||||||||||||||||||||||||||||||||||||||||||||||||||||||||||||||||||||||||

# Biblical Essentials
# for Teamwork in Christ

SHERWOOD G. LINGENFELTER

In chapters 1 and 2, we examined two case studies (Julie's and the apostle Paul's) of how members of two respective ministry teams struggled with commitments to ways of life so severely divergent that the members rejected one another, broke into factions, and even sought to undermine the ministry of the others on their team. The bad news is that such fragmentation is frequent among Christians who seek to do "mission with" each other in obedience to Christ. The good news is that Paul's experience in Antioch—and later in his church plants—so provoked him that he wrote his Epistles to the Thessalonians, Galatians, and Philippians to equip Christians to engage and resolve these problems in Christ. The purpose of this chapter is to summarize what we believe are the biblical essentials available to Christian workers when—led by the Holy Spirit—they seek the spiritual power and pathways to engage and frame "clumsy," but Christ-filled, solutions to such problems. We will then apply these essentials to our analysis of Julie's crisis and the crises faced by the contributing authors in part 3 of this book.

## Centered on the Cross—Mission in Weakness

> Our global organization inadvertently fosters a competitiveness that is visible on the field. On the surface it does not seem harmful, but over time it can turn into jealousy, comparison, bringing others down to size, and maintaining *my spot* in the pecking order.[1]

Most mission organizations face this human habit of competition inherent in our relationships with one another, which leads to the temptations of comparison, jealousy, and sin. Small sins lead to greater self-reliance and seeking to do mission from our respective positions of strength. The apostle Paul defines his and our mission to the nations in terms of the weakness of the cross.[2] "For I resolved to know nothing while I was with you except Jesus Christ and him crucified. I came to you in weakness with great fear and trembling" (1 Cor. 2:2–3). Christ crucified provides the theological ground for "mission with" from this position of weakness; unless we are willing to surrender our obsessions with organization, competition, rivalry, and our pecking orders, we cannot fulfill God's calling and purpose. Like the peoples of Corinth and Galatia, twenty-first-century Christians remain in the world and face the same question: What does it mean for us—living and working in the world context—to be transformed into the image of Christ?

Multinational mission teams suffer from the same human weaknesses of their sending churches and organizations. Paul makes it clear that Christ crucified, and Christ alone, is the source of our acceptance before God, and his death on the cross created the possibility for our response of faith: "You irrational Galatians [Americans, Brits, Germans, Indians, Chinese, Thais]! Who put a spell on you? Jesus Christ was put on display as crucified before your eyes! . . . Did you

---

1. Elizabeth McLean (pseudonym), interview by Sherwood G. Lingenfelter, December 2, 2020.
2. Jeong, "Essence of Leadership," 127–28.

receive the Spirit by doing the works of the Law or by believing what
you heard? Are you so irrational? After you started with the Spirit,
are you now finishing up with your own human effort?" (Gal. 3:1–3
CEB). Peter admonishes us, "You were redeemed from the empty
way of life handed down to you from your ancestors . . . with the
precious blood of Christ, a lamb without blemish or defect" (1 Pet.
1:18–19). It is on this ground alone that we are able to set aside the
"empty way of life" that we have acquired simply by being born into
a family, community, and nation.

We must understand from the outset that the cross overturns all
our cultural patterns of identity, authority, and values for personal,
family, and public life. For example, Paul rebukes the church in Corinth
for internal factions and for its obsession with wisdom, philosophy,
and partisan politics. Paul challenges the Corinthian Christians—
people of the flesh—to reorient their understanding of leadership
to a theology of the cross. He rebukes them by recounting his own
leadership and declaring himself a fool for Christ (1 Cor. 4:10).

## Centered "in Christ," Not "in the World"—Habits of Life

What do we mean by "in the world"? For most readers of this book,
the first criterion is education. If you are reading this, you have likely
achieved a level of education that is above the average for persons
in your community. Education usually is oriented toward careers, so
perhaps you have chosen or are considering a career related to the
church and God's mission. Very likely you drive a car and live in a
house with electricity and its many conveniences. You have learned
habits about authority in the home and at work, about how to control
your life in such a way that you achieve your goals and aspirations
for success. We consider most of these things essential for our lives,
and we tend to reproduce them wherever we live and work.

In all of his writings, Paul speaks of the dawn of a new age foretold
in the Old Testament—the arrival of the Messiah, the crucifixion of
Christ, and the outpouring of the Holy Spirit.[3] In his theology, the

3. Russell, *In the World but Not of the World*, 137–38.

crucifixion and resurrection of Christ marks the end of the old and the beginning of the new. The gift of the Holy Spirit to those who believe confirms God's fulfillment of the promise and the beginning of new life "in the Spirit" as we live in expectation of Christ's return. Thus Paul's charge: As "children of the light and children of the day," he says, "let us not be like others, who are asleep, but let us be awake and sober. . . . Let us be sober, putting on faith and love as a breastplate, and the hope of salvation as a helmet" (1 Thess. 5:5–6, 8).

Therefore, the challenge for us in this book is this: How do we live as "children of the light"—awake, sober, and putting on faith, love, and hope—and engage in teamwork cross-culturally until Christ comes again? We are living as Christ-followers between Christ's resurrection and his triumphal return. So this is a time of significant ambiguity! How do we live "in the world" when our loyalty and calling are "in Christ" rather than to the pattern of life lived by those who do not know Christ and who order their lives by customs related to jobs, marriage, extended family, and political loyalties? What does it mean to live as "children of the light"? Elizabeth McLean describes her experience this way:

> In order to combat this, we must become a filter through which new members experience an in-Christ team committed to in-Christ responses to the world's culture and to our own organizational culture. The only way to achieve such transformation is through "immersion in Scripture"—a "word filter" that screens out the fruit of the flesh. As leaders, we have failed them on more than one occasion—sometimes not giving people a fair assessment or a fair opportunity to grow—thus denying them the opportunity for growth by experiencing in-Christ community.[4]

## One Body, a Household of Faith, the Temple of God—Team Metaphors

The outworking of this new identity in Christ for cross-cultural teamwork is guided by the metaphors used by Paul: one body, a household

4. Elizabeth McLean, interview.

of faith, and the temple of God. The "one body" metaphor is elaborated in many places in Paul's writings, but we will give particular attention to Ephesians. I have argued elsewhere that the power of a church, mission organization, or multinational team is directly related to its capacity to function as one body; when the people of God work together in the unity of the Spirit, they have the capacity to attain "the whole measure of the fullness of Christ" (Eph. 4:13).[5] The body works best when it represents the diversity of individuals that the Holy Spirit brings together for God's mission.

Paul also makes the point that Christ, and Christ alone, is head—and Christ does his work through those he has gifted for service. In light of this fact, we must rethink what we mean when we speak of leadership in any context for the body of Christ, and particularly within a multinational team.

> The fundamental lesson for [team] leadership here is that "body work" is counter-cultural. It is not about structure, role and rules. Rather, our most important functional role is made clear in Ephesians 4:16; the most visible spiritual gifts—apostles, prophets, evangelists, pastors and teachers—serve as supporting ligaments, so that the body grows, and that every part does its work. This truth is so important, yet so counter to most cultural understandings of leadership. We prefer structure, roles, and rules.[6]

In this book we will examine how the team leaders function in one body to support every member of a team in such a way that each part does its work.

The family and household metaphor occurs in all of Paul's Epistles, and this metaphor is probably the most important for cross-cultural teamwork. Our identity in Christ creates a significant shift in the nature and character of our relationships with others. Those who are in Christ share a new horizontal structure of relationships as brothers and sisters in Christ. The sibling relationship is cited more than 118 times in Paul's Letters.[7] The source of these relationships

5. Lingenfelter, *Leadership in the Way of the Cross*, 100.
6. Lingenfelter, *Leadership in the Way of the Cross*, 102.
7. Russell, *In the World but Not of the World*, 152.

is God: "There is one body and one Spirit, just as you were called to one hope when you were called; one Lord, one faith, one baptism; one God and Father of all, who is over all and through all and in all" (Eph. 4:4–6).

As with "one body," family and household are not culturally specific concepts but rather a transformation of "in the world" statuses and how we connect with them in our communities. Galatians 3:28 makes it clear that categories of insider-outsider, hierarchies of master-slave, and gender divisions are overturned in Christ. For teamwork, that means nation of origin, status of prior occupation, wealth or poverty of family of origin, and position in a mission organization are all overturned in Christ. For example, Robert and Elizabeth McLean (authors of chap. 11) redefined their titles and roles from "directors of training" to servants and shepherds. Their expectations of teamwork include sharing meals; affection lived out in respect, honor, and caring for one another; protecting members from adversaries and correcting when needed; and harmony and peace in team relationships with one another.

Finally, when we build a multinational team around the metaphor "temple of God," we locate our identity and accountability at the center of who we are and who we serve—"in him you too are being built together to become a dwelling in which God lives by his Spirit" (Eph. 2:22). For example, mission leader Martins Atanda (author of chap. 13) writes about teamwork with local people for local and regional outreach in Central and North Africa. He and "core team" members work hard to build up local leadership and to empower these people to follow the core team members' example as they (the leaders) follow Christ. By gathering people for prayer and worship—which cycles from the "core team" to regional and international teams—they renew their reliance on the power of Jesus to heal, forgive, and lead people into an abundant and eternal life.

These three metaphors—one body, a household of faith, the temple of God—capture what it means to be in Christ and yet live and serve within a world that has all the structures—family, social class, economic status, positions, values, and interests—that distort and fracture human social and economic life. When we recognize God at the core of everything we are and do, we are then accountable, as Paul writes, to "love one another" (Rom. 13:8), to "submit to one another out of reverence for Christ" (Eph. 5:21), and to work together in "the unity of the Spirit through the bond of peace" (4:3).

Finally, "servant" is the universal role for all followers of Christ, whatever role they may play in a team's social and ministry context. No one who is serious about following Jesus can ignore Jesus's words in Luke 22:25–27: "The kings of the Gentiles lord it over them; and those who exercise authority over them call themselves Benefactors. But you are not to be like that. Instead, the greatest among you should be like the youngest, and the one who rules like the one who serves. For who is greater, the one who is at the table or the one who serves? Is it not the one who is at the table? But I am among you as one who serves."

## Work of Faith, Labor of Love, Steadfast Hope: Household Living

> We always give thanks to God for all of you and mention you in our prayers, constantly remembering before our God and Father your *work of faith and labor of love and steadfastness of hope* in our Lord Jesus Christ. (1 Thess. 1:2–3 NRSV)

> The triad of faith, hope and love plays an important part in Pauline ethics, . . . and [these] are the continuing responses of a community under duress, . . . a comprehensive description of Christian existence.[8]

We have already seen that teamwork is best understood by the metaphor "household of faith." We next turn to see what Paul tells us about household life. The "work of faith" is an absolutely essential ingredient in person and team formation. Faith is not something that just happens—it is a gift from God that must be nurtured to maturity both in the life of the individual and in the life of the community. As Paul describes it, faith is a "continuing response to the Gospel"[9] in our relationship with God the Father, Christ, and others.

8. Thompson, *Apostle of Persuasion*, 112.
9. Thompson, *Apostle of Persuasion*, 113.

The work of faith is always the "orientation toward Christ."[10]
Christ's death, resurrection, and exaltation were and are *for us*—
sinners and rebels against God. Faith is believing in him, trusting in
him, abiding in him, and—in allegiance to him—obeying his com-
mandments. Such work includes the disciplines of prayer, reading
Scripture, and seeking to obey what we have understood so that we
may "bring to fruition [our] every desire for goodness and [our] every
deed prompted by faith" (2 Thess. 1:11). But the most important
insight for teamwork is that this work of faith is both an individual
and a collective work. One sort of work without the other is inadequate, because each is essential for the household to reach maturity
in Christ and to respond as a community under duress.

When I (Sherwood) reflect on my own habits and experience, I find
that doubt, lack, and weakness are often present in my trust relationship with God. My doubts come from anxiety about things going on
around me, questions about my own competence and that of others,
fear about the adequacy of what I and they know and believe, and
concerns about the viability of my and our plans or strategy—all of
which get in the way of my and our faith. So it is essential for effective
teamwork for all members to do the work of faith—the most important part of which is to reorient ourselves toward Christ: individually
and together repenting, praying in the Spirit, and trusting God in the
midst of individual and collective doubt.

We will explore many examples of the work of faith in parts 2 and 3
of this book. Perhaps the most important thought before we do this
is to understand the diversity of the households. In our case studies,
no two of the teams do the work of faith in the same way, and within
each team, no two individuals do the work of faith in the same way.
Christians are all called by Christ and invited into a relationship with
him, and in their unique personalities, personal histories, and team col-
lectives they respond to Christ and to one another in often unique and
wonderful ways. We encourage you to watch for this as you read further.

The "labor of love" is the second component of household life as
persons and as a team. Love is not just an emotional state of being

10. Thompson, *Apostle of Persuasion*, 222.

that flows out of happiness or a specific attraction to others. The love that Paul is speaking of is intentional action—deeds of goodness prompted by faith. First Corinthians 13 shows that love involves many very specific kinds of actions: Love is patient and kind; love bears, believes, hopes, and endures all things. Love is *not* envious, boastful, arrogant, rude, irritable, or resentful, nor does it rejoice in wrongdoing. It is no surprise, then, that Paul speaks of the labor of love.

The point here is that love does not flow naturally from who we are as people. Rather, the labor of love requires us to be intentional about our relationships and to nurture spiritual qualities in our responses to others. Colossians 3 reminds us that love flows when we—individually and collectively—"put on" or cultivate attitudes of compassion, kindness, humility, gentleness, and patience. Paul admonishes us to "bear with each other and forgive one another" (v. 13) even as Christ has forgiven us. And then he charges the Colossians and us to "over all these virtues put on love, which binds them all together in perfect unity" (v. 14). The labor of love is something we must intentionally do to be effective within our households of faith and as we share the gospel with others.

The "steadfastness of hope" (1 Thess. 1:3 NRSV) is the third component of team and personal living. Paul grounds our hope in the promise of Christ's return and our calling to be faithful servants until he comes again. The circumstances for this admonition include persecution and suffering (1:6) as individuals and as a team. In chapter 13, Martins Atanda illustrates how similar situations continue to play out in modern mission contexts. In his ministry in Central Africa, Atanda and his core team members experienced much opposition—police roadblocks, eight team members kept overnight in prison, closed churches, and threats of violence. In many places, they experienced hard ground and resistance to their ministries of help and hope. However, they persisted—even in the most hostile contexts—to offer their work of faith and labor of love. God's blessing and assurance enabled them to persevere.

Steadfast hope for cross-cultural teamwork emanates from the glory of the cross and the anticipation of Christ's continuing redemptive works of service—among us and through us—in spite of opposition and even persecution.

Our conclusion as we look at the complexities of wicked problems and teamwork is that the triad of faith, love, and hope is critical in our personal and team lives and essential to our success as households of faith. As we reflect on the case study of Paul's wicked problem in Antioch, it seems evident that James, Peter, and Barnabas failed to trust God in the crisis, when they were forced to choose between loving gentiles such as Titus and Timothy—accepting them at table fellowship—and conforming to the pressures of the Jerusalem faction. When we lose trust in God's presence and holiness, we default to the pressures of the social and theological expectations of those around us. Without the works of faith in our personal and household living, without the labor of love in our relationships within the team and toward others that we serve, and lacking steadfastness of hope, we will surely fall short of being counted *worthy of the kingdom* of God.

## REFLECTION QUESTIONS

- As you reflect on these "biblical essentials," do they lead you to the conclusion that we must understand our teamwork as "mission from a position of weakness"? If so, how?
- Has your understanding of "in the world but not of the world" changed after reading this chapter? If so, how?
- In what way do the three biblical metaphors—one body, a household of faith, the temple of God—stretch your understanding of what it means to do "mission with" diverse members of the global church?
- How does the discussion of the work of faith and the labor of love stretch your understanding of what it means to serve on a multinational team, sharing Christ in cultural contexts other than your own?

# PART 2

# "In the World" Deceptions and Disagreements

The world is indeed dangerous, and when we commit to work together in multinational teams, our virtues in Christ are often tested to the point at which our fears override our virtues. The history of mission organizations experimenting with cross-cultural teamwork has scores of stories of pain, suffering, and fear of risk and failure. In most of these cases, the greatest challenges to unity were internal, arising from deeply held but conflicting values of team members and fundamental disagreements about legitimate processes for making decisions and about the rules of the game that govern the daily work of teams.

The goal of part 2 is to equip readers to discern and respond "in Christ" to six areas of "in the world" deceptions that challenge leaders and team members. Chapters 4 through 6 address organizational challenges: management, problem solving, and return on investment. Chapters 7 through 9 explore interpersonal tensions: values conflicts, personality needs or hungers, and spiritual self-deception.

Julie opens the discussion in chapters 4 and 5, illustrating how uncertainty about power and authority and our attachments to "my way of life" and "my elegant solution" lead team leaders and members deep into conflict with one another and lead to the death of their vision in a "wicked problem."

I (Sherwood) follow in chapters 6 through 9, drawing on data from the case studies of the contributing authors that will follow in chapters 10 through 13 to explore four additional issues of "in the world" deceptions, including both organizational and interpersonal issues. In each chapter, I compare data from two case studies related to the specific issue of that chapter. Chapter 6 asks what language we use to talk about ministry returns or harvest; the cases compared are those of Matthew Crosland (chapter 12) and Martins Atanda (chapter 13). Chapter 7 asks whether you can disagree and yet work together; the cases compared are those of Penny Bakewell (chapter 10) and Crosland (chapter 12). Chapter 8 asks what the tensions are between personal identity, role, and in-Christ relationships; the cases compared are those of Bakewell (chapter 10) and Robert and Elizabeth McLean (chapter 11). Chapter 9 asks how we must balance convictions, rights, and love in Christ in a team context; the cases compared are those of the McLeans (chapter 11) and Atanda (chapter 13).

These questions may not be exhaustive but are prevalent within our contributing cases. I have presented the analysis before the chapters describing the actual cases (which can be found in part 3) with enough summary detail that you will not need to refer to part 3 while reading part 2. However, chapters 10 through 13 do include the full story of each case study, and I hope that my analysis in this section will prepare you for reading the actual cases so that they contribute even more to your deep reflection and possible application as someone engaged in teamwork cross-culturally.

# 4

‖‖‖‖‖‖‖‖‖‖‖‖‖‖‖‖‖‖‖‖‖‖‖‖‖‖‖‖‖‖‖‖‖‖‖‖‖‖‖‖‖‖‖‖‖‖‖‖‖‖‖‖‖‖‖‖‖‖‖‖‖‖‖‖‖‖‖‖‖‖‖‖‖‖‖‖‖‖‖‖‖‖‖

# Uncertainty about Power and Authority

## JULIE A. GREEN

My Dear Wormwood, . . . The sense of ownership in general is always to be encouraged. The humans are always putting up claims to ownership which sound equally funny in Heaven and in Hell and we must keep them doing so. . . . We teach them not to notice the different senses of the possessive pronoun—the finely graded differences that run from "my boots" through "my dog", "my servant", "my wife", "my father", "my master" and "my country", to "my God". They can be taught to reduce all of these senses to that of "my boots", and the "my" of ownership. . . . And all the time the joke is that the word "Mine" in its fully possessive sense cannot be uttered by a human being about anything.[1]

The complexities of "wicked problems" make decision-making so unpredictable that they overturn standard practices of leadership and management. The objective of this chapter is to show how "my" deeply held cultural values about authority and team decision-making

1. Lewis, *Screwtape Letters*, 108–9.

create a wicked problem for teams and leaders. Working from this case, we examine the spectrum of leadership strategies for critical, tame, and wicked problems. We then offer guidance for multinational team leaders on how to address "in Christ" the uncertainty about power and authority that is endemic to their teamwork.

## Uncertainty about Power and Authority: A Case Study

As I (Julie) shared in chapter 1, my Southeast Asia language development team (SAT) was angry with me and resisted anything I proposed. My team rejected the way I had processed a decision to go forward and dismissed my proposal since it failed to achieve the organizational revolt against SIL International, our sponsoring organization, that so many of my team members desired.

Using my authority and power as team leader, I had first interviewed the team members in person to hear their thoughts about working with SIL. Then, after they returned to their language allocation areas, I had written the strategic framework document based on strategic thinking and my felt need to compromise. Once I finished the document, the next step was to invite the team to provide feedback and discuss the document by email. In a flood of complaining and condemning emails, the field teams of SAT took turns tearing down my proposed strategy. As I processed these emails, I discovered that their critiques were grounded in what I had learned were their preferred "ways of life" (see fig. 4.1).

One couple, who followed an "authority rules" way of life (which accepts top-down power over members), said that they were okay with whatever I outlined because I was their leader. I just needed to tell them what to do, and they would follow whatever I said. Another team member, who preferred the hierarchy way of life (which shares power between the group and its leaders), said that he would not work with SAT. He felt that the national organization did not value quality language work.

A team member who followed the individualist way of life (in which individuals hold independent power) said that he would immediately

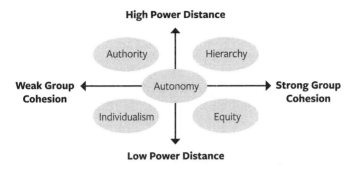

**Figure 4.1** Five ways of life, two dimensions of sociality
Adapted from Michael Thompson, Richard Ellis, and Aaron B. Wildavsky, *Cultural Theory, Political Cultures* (Boulder, CO: Westview, 1990), 8.

resign from the team and start a separate language development organization in the country where he was working. A fourth team member, who preferred the equity way of life (in which group consensus overrules individual members), stated that she could not follow the plan. She was offended because persons with the right language fluency and technical experience were not a part of the creation of the strategy. After the team members communicated with one another, it was not long before they rejected any plan that included remaining in SIL. They wanted out (autonomy), and they wanted the freedom to do projects their way.

The rule patterns we have seen in these diverse responses to the SAT crisis may be summarized as follows:

1. Authority rules: the powerless are vulnerable to those in power—an isolated and fatalistic way of life (I will do what you say).

2. Hierarchy rules: dissent must be managed by authority within the group and can be controlled—an engaged and controlling way of life (I want to be part of a group that respects authority and works with it).

3. Individual rules: social risk is normal and essential to the mission—an engaged and optimistic way of life (I will resign and start anew with others who will take the risks).

4. Equity rules: dissent is threat, is unacceptable, and must be stopped—an engaged and fearful way of life (people like me are excluded; we need people who can agree).

Once I understood these polarizing positions of my teammates, I knew there was no right answer about how to make decisions on this team. I had run into a sticky, wicked problem without understanding it, and my desire to use "my authority" to control the process and create certainty was making it worse.

## The Leadership Challenge in Wicked Problems

My leadership challenge in this case study is not only typical but rather common to leaders of multinational teams. When team members come from many different cultural backgrounds and various organizational cultures, the tension over "my or your values" will always be high and the path forward uncertain. All who try to lead in such circumstances must deal with uncertainty; no one can honestly know the future. Yet team members expect the leader to work with them to shape the future. Everyone becomes anxious about the tension and inertia, and the burden of taming uncertainty so the organization can move forward falls on its leader. So how does the one who picks up this burden carry it in a way that manages the uncertainty? In other words, how can one be valued as a "good" leader?

To answer this question, it is helpful to look at the relationships between uncertainty, the types of problems leaders are facing, and the decision-making processes available to them. Scholar Keith Grint is very helpful for this, showing us that there is a clear correlation between an increasing degree of uncertainty and the degree of wickedness of a problem.[2] Grint suggests that different types of problems—critical, tame-complex, wicked—demand leadership actions to engage the people involved and create a pathway toward a solution to the problem (see fig. 4.2).

2. Grint, "Problems, Problems, Problems," 1473.

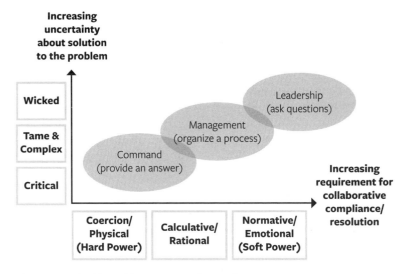

**Figure 4.2** Leadership: problems, power, and uncertainty

Adapted from Keith Grint, "Wicked Problems and Clumsy Solutions: The Role of Leadership," in *The New Public Leadership Challenge*, ed. Stephen Brookes and Keith Grint (New York: Palgrave Macmillan, 2010), 180.

Grint suggests that the problems with the most straightforward solutions are the critical problems, such as a fire in a building. The level of uncertainty is minimal, and a leader is expected to use command-and-control authority in such circumstances. Leaders often solve these problems by using power and, at times, even force or coercion (see fig. 4.2). In my case, the typical critical problem was scheduling meetings with the language development teams. As the language development team leader, I did not have to negotiate to schedule time for a meeting, since we had already agreed to a monthly calendar. To make the meeting happen, I only had to coordinate the logistics for the meeting and send a confirmation announcement to the language development team.

Tame problems are more complex, involving a degree of uncertainty, but management processes are in place to lower or mitigate the risk of the unknown. For example, when creating budgets, leaders gather data, such as historical spending and income trends, to reduce their uncertainty and help them make the right decision. Tame problems can be solved through established management processes.

The risk for leaders of multinational teams is applying management strategies to resolve issues that are not actually "tame," such as I did in the case study above. When I talked with the SIL leaders and board about starting language development projects, we saw the problem as technical (tame). Both the SIL leaders and I had started projects before, and we thought we knew what it took. However, we wrongly assumed that we could solve the problem between my SAT members and SIL by applying management processes.

The wicked problems are the last and most challenging in Grint's typology (see fig. 4.2). The essence of a wicked problem is that both the problem and the solution are fundamentally unknowable. As we saw in my case study, a wicked problem brings to light conflicting values and contested processes. It is impossible to find the right answer to satisfy even most team members, and uncertainty about the problem only increases as leaders try to "manage the problem."

Grint suggests that the only recourse for leaders is to apply what he terms "soft power" to "ask the right questions rather than provide the right answers because the answers may not be self-evident and will require a collaborative process to make any kind of progress."[3] Soft power engages the emotional and normative behaviors of participants, mediating differences among followers so that they are motivated to listen to one another and to compromise. Usually this requires a relationship and face-to-face work so that people see and experience the other individuals in the room. Hard words and opinions shared in email or other written communication are much less effective and take far more time. Even with collaboration, a wicked problem is rarely, if ever, solved, because one solution gives birth to another problem.

It is remarkable that Grint, a secular scholar, recognizes what we, followers of Christ, have known from the beginning of our faith in Jesus; the new commandment given to us in Christ is to "love one another." Paul further commands us to engage in the work of faith and the labor of love. So the mystery is why we resist this. Why do we revert to our own authority and power? As Screwtape reminds us so graphically, we focus on "my" values, "my" agenda, and "my" solutions.[4]

3. Grint, "Problems, Problems, Problems," 1473.
4. Lewis, *Screwtape Letters*, 108–9.

## Managing by "My" Authority and Power

In the case of SAT, I created a framework for starting new projects in an attempt to lower the uncertainty and risks involved in that process. When I received criticism from the team, I approached it as a technical problem. Similarly, the SIL board assumed that starting language development projects was a problem for which the SIL leadership could formulate a reasoned, thoughtful solution after receiving the right information (i.e., that it was a tame problem). Anticipating such a solution, the board gave me time to research the problem and report back. I came to the conclusion that the issue had multiple known solutions and that it was my job to figure out which was most appropriate. The SIL board and language development staff then could use my framework as a draft proposal for further discussion.

I understood my role as that of a manager, managing processes and ideas, rather than that of a leader, asking questions and profoundly engaging with team members to discover whether and when they might follow. I heard and understood the value differences between the SIL staff and the language development staff. The gaps were significant, but I thought I could manage them with the right proposal. I did not recognize the level of collaboration needed, so I did not use soft power, or in-Christ engagement, to help my team members reconcile their differences with SIL. Of course, this only made the problem worse.

The SIL board collaborated with me, endorsing my false assumptions. The board members also assumed they knew the essentials needed to start new language projects. They too thought that the problem was tame and that we could use a management process to solve it. They did not recognize the significant value differences present within the board and staff. These value differences required the "soft power" of listening, reflecting, and then asking questions to lead people toward collaboration with SAT language development teams.

Finally, the individual SAT language development workers all thought they knew how to solve the problem of starting language development projects. However, as they heard each other's opinions, they rejected the ideas they did not like and built coalitions with the teammates whose views were similar. My proposal further entrenched and divided the team into like-minded groups. Together we created a wicked problem that we could not resolve separately.

## A Fractured Team—"My Way" Apart from Christ

Multinational teams that are fractured by wicked problems experience three stages in team development: forming, storming, and norming. The commonality that draws members together is usually enough to get them through the forming stage. Initially, they may move quickly to the storming stage as each member brings "my" unique and divergent ideas to the team. However, they typically get stuck in the "storming stage,"[5] and unfortunately, the norming stage does not come as easily. The variety of competing logics in the team make it very difficult to negotiate a common team culture and way of doing things—so often, in desperation, a single "elegant" win-lose decision is made, and the team fractures even more. Worse, if team members are Christians, they often resist conversations about who we are in Christ, accusing one another of trying to spiritualize the problem.

In the case study, these "kingdom workers" illustrate how a wicked problem fractured both SAT—the language development team—and SIL—the supporting organization. My SAT members easily moved from the forming to the storming stage of team development, but they had a hard time putting down their own interests and engaging with the "other interests" of the SIL leaders. When we refused to engage in dialogue during the storming stage of development, we failed to negotiate a common and agreed-upon way of working together. So, while we had committed to God's mission of language development and translation, we never spoke about our spiritual identity as the body of Christ. SAT divided into subgroups in revolt; some threatened to create a new organization, while others wanted to stay with SIL. Similarly, the SIL staff fractured into groups—some were willing to work with the SAT language development staff, and others gave up trying. As the team leader, I saw the win-lose nature of the challenge,

5. Tuckman, "Developmental Sequence in Small Groups," 390.

and, while I was uncomfortable with it, my efforts to move the team forward with my "in the world" proposal failed.

## "In the World" Authority: "Mission with" Implodes

In this chapter, we have shown how the blessed diversity of multinational teams—the body of Christ in action for God's mission to the world—implodes when we—in pride about "my way" of life and "my certainty" about how things should be done—insist that partnership and teamwork be done by "my authority" in "my way." As you read the story, you found nothing about the "work of faith and labor of love and steadfastness of hope" (1 Thess. 1:3 NRSV). All of that was forgotten or—worse—relegated to our private lives and denied in our "job" and public "job-related" relationships. This is a common curse of diverse Western cultures—we fear allowing our faith to interfere with or intrude into our daily work or public relationships!

Further, we have learned that multinational teams and partnerships between organizations, called by God for his global mission, cannot take for granted any of our individual and collective way-of-life assumptions. Doing so will produce problems in our mission and work so intractable that the act of trying to solve them by a linear process—a planning model that calls for researching the problem, designing a solution, implementing it, and testing it—will only make them worse. These problems are "wicked" not only in their unforgiving cultural complexity and contradictions of differing opinions but also in our inherent propensity for judgment and moral condemnation of those who approach the issues differently from us. By yielding to such condemnation of others, we disobey our Lord Jesus Christ, who commanded that, in our practice of ministry and in our personal lives, we love our neighbors as ourselves.

It took me and the SAT language development team more than two years to recover from our inability to identify and address the wicked problem of creating a partnership strategy with SIL to start shared language development projects. The interpersonal damage we did to each other was significant, and the damage we did to God's kingdom work was extensive, as believers and nonbelievers alike watched our sinful interactions with each other. Hurtful words had been spoken, disrespectful emails sent, and much face had been lost. It was a difficult and painful process, but in the end, through much prayer as well as mediation by believers from outside the team, the Spirit guided us through forgiveness to godly relationships with each other. And, by God's great mercy, when I left Southeast Asia to return to my home country, the team members were once again coworkers and friends.

In the chapters that follow, we assume that multinational teamwork and partnerships, because of the very nature of their diversity, have the potential to turn all types of collaborative work into "wicked problems." At the same time, we understand—from the positive cases by our contributing authors—that when we live and work "in Christ," the Spirit of God works among us and through us to help us lead and follow in ways that glorify God and bring joy and blessing to those we lead and serve. Further, in-Christ solutions to wicked problems are not "authority focused" or "returns focused" but rather focused on the body of Christ and the temple of God. We will thus explore alternatives for leaders and followers to ask new questions, to think in fresh ways about answers, to create biblically informed networks of relationship, and to construct ad hoc practices to work together in each unique situation as diverse members of the global church.

## REFLECTION QUESTIONS

- Can you identify a "wicked problem" in your teamwork?
- What made this a wicked problem?
- Who were the differing and contrary voices? What values did they represent?
- To what extent did the team focus on "in the world" authority and solutions?
- To what extent did the team seek the direction of the Holy Spirit and in-Christ authority and solutions?

# 5

# The Deception of Elegant Solutions

JULIE A. GREEN

In chapter 4, I (Julie) reported how I interviewed my team members on the Southeast Asia Team (SAT) to learn about their prior experiences working with their sponsoring organization (SIL). After those interviews, I reported my findings to the leaders of SIL and discussed with them the issues my team members had raised. Once we had processed this information, I decided to develop a "strategic framework" of next steps, which I then presented to my SAT members. As I reported, the result of my presentation was a disaster—the team members' reactions surprised and then dismayed me as they completely rejected my elegant "strategic framework."

The members of SAT and SIL were facing a wicked problem: we had voiced multiple and conflicting opinions about strategy and solutions for language development. Had I ignored this challenge, as the "authority rules" couple suggested, I would have dismissed the viewpoints of the other team members, who all refused any suggestion of further engagement with SIL leadership. Further, two members had serious reservations about working with the others on SAT. If SIL were to choose any one of the SAT members' counterstrategies, that solution would change the very nature of the problem, and it would morph into a new and more complex problem for the team to handle. When team members find themselves in such a contradictory predicament, where should a leader look for solutions?

### Elegant Solutions: The "Perfect" Response?

Elegant solutions are solutions that seem to be the right choice *because* they are elegant. I felt that my "strategic framework" was a perfect response to my teammates' reservations about working with SIL and with each other. It seemed obvious to me: as the leader seeking to bring them together, the logic made sense.

As I have since reflected on this situation, I have concluded that leaders choose elegant solutions because, as they evaluate all the known possibilities, one solution looks and sounds like the best way forward. With tame and technical types of problems, this strategy usually works reasonably well. However, in situations such as the one I faced, ignoring the competing realities within my team and choosing an elegant solution only compounded the problem. It actually precipitated a reaction from SAT members that morphed into a more significant wicked problem.

Let us look more closely at the debate within my team about solutions. One team member, who follows an individualist way of life, had no interest in resolving the conflicts. He was confident that he could start his own organization and do a better job of language program development. He didn't need others; he would find people like himself who just wanted the freedom to frame their own program options.

Others, who embrace a hierarchy way of life, were concerned about controlling the quality of language work, and they felt that the members of SAT did not share their values. They wanted to withdraw from SAT and seek to work with SIL people who would advocate for investing in and protecting the quality appropriate for translating the Word of God.

The member who prefers the equity way of life was offended because she—a person with the "right" language fluency and technical experience—was not included in the creation of the strategy. She felt that her approach to language development would enable the team to best serve each language group to meet the particular needs and interests related to its own language. She refused to support the strategic framework, which she felt was a solution inadequate for the challenges facing the team.

While the couple who embraced the "authority rules" way of life agreed to the plan, they were not committed, only compliant. They believed that no one really cared what they thought, so it was useless to engage in a way that might jeopardize their membership and calling.

The expectation of the members of SAT was that any team leader should be able to understand and empathize with the values underlying each way of life embraced by the diverse team members. Further, any team leader must be adept at helping members negotiate and do the same. They understood and rejected my solution as "scissors"—cutting their specific ideas. Similarly, the team members who stubbornly sought to impose their own solutions to the wicked problem only made the problem worse, because they alienated one another and rejected collaboration.

## Surprise!

One of the first steps toward "solving" a wicked problem is to recognize the telltale sign of a wicked problem: surprise! Team leaders encountering a wicked problem are inevitably surprised—as I was—when others challenge their default logic for solving a problem. It is easy for a leader to ignore this initial surprise—as I tried to do—because a challenge to their logic seems irrational. Ignoring the surprise, however, can be fatal, since it is a signal that values are clashing.

This value clash is at the heart of the wicked problem. Leaders who can recognize the surprise and begin to understand the reasoning behind the solution put themselves and their team in a learning stance. Team members and leaders who do not acknowledge surprise as a symptom of the problem run the risk of making the problem worse by either ignoring the issue or responding out of their culture-based judgment system.[1]

Fortunately, we have hope amid the chaos and mess of multinational teamwork, because the responsibility for and results of our work ultimately belong to the Lord. Further, he is our just and good supervisor. When we are inclined to listen, he gives us the Holy Spirit to be our meek leader's ultimate guide. He is the only one who can manage the planning and uncertainty of doing God's mission.

## Stumbling into a "Clumsy Solution"

> Clumsy solutions come about when multiple, diverse, perhaps incompatible, perspectives are brought to bear on an issue, resulting in a settlement that is inelegant from any single perspective, but robust because it relies on more than one epistemological and ethical foundation.[2]

Drawing on the works of secular scholars on wicked problems, I have concluded that to find a viable, reasonable "clumsy solution" to a wicked problem, multinational team leaders must first resist the temptation to search for single answers and to take pride in elegant or straightforward solutions. Instead, they must lead their team so that members (1) tolerate those who disagree with their own simple, even elegant solutions and (2) embrace the discomfort of contrary views about knowledge and embrace the logic that leads to "nonsensical" responses to the crisis. Such tolerance and listening do not come naturally to anyone. Our upbringing and cultural values provide us with preferences that are hidden (to us), knowledge about what constitutes the right solution, and hatred for other ways of solving problems. As Screwtape reminds us, "The word 'Mine' in its fully possessive sense cannot be uttered by a human being about anything."[3]

But it is even more important to understand who we are "in Christ" and to build in Christ on the wisdom of others who have sought to

---

1. For a more detailed treatment of this subject, see Silzer, *Biblical Multicultural Teams*.
2. Rayner, "Uncomfortable Knowledge," 123.
3. Lewis, *Screwtape Letters*, 109.

understand how to lead in wicked problem situations. To be clumsy, I will have to resist in Christ the temptation and pride of being seen by others as a wise and decisive leader. I need to humble myself in Christ to lead this team through a process of deep listening to one another. We will need to listen to each other in Christ in ways that allow each team member both to be heard and to affect the solution. Then we need the "labor of love"—engaging in dialogue with one another, listening to the Holy Spirit, and seeking to find the way of Christ in this challenging situation. This process is complicated because "my" cultural values encase the behaviors and actions that are considered right (and wrong). And competent leadership in one culture may be deemed poor leadership in another. Team leaders must also learn to listen to each other's logical solutions to the problem without immediately judging the answers as inadequate or ineffective. Clumsiness requires that team members hear and understand the values that are embedded in each other's solutions and accept them as valid and *incomplete*.

### Confronting Uncomfortable Knowledge

What is uncomfortable knowledge? Uncomfortable knowledge is knowledge that challenges our prior understanding of a situation. It is the knowledge that makes a wicked problem more complicated than we want to believe, the knowledge that overturns a value or principle we have taken for granted, and the knowledge that leads us in a direction that we do not want to go. Because our world is complicated, to make sense of it, leaders tend to simplify complex issues into a self-consistent version of the world. This process automatically excludes any messy, inconsistent bits of a problem. Leaders and institutions must resist using the strategies of denial, dismissal, diversion, and displacement to keep uncomfortable knowledge away from the forefront[4] and must bring these messy bits of the problem out into the open. It is only in this way that they can begin to follow Jesus in such complexity. These messy bits of an issue are essential if

4. Rayner, "Uncomfortable Knowledge."

a leader is going to stumble upon an in-Christ solution that requires the labor of love. If a leader does not embrace the complicated and sometimes chaotic, uncomfortable knowledge inherent in the problem, the unacknowledged knowledge will compound the problem and undermine any elegant solution.

I and my SAT teammates in the case study had to embrace the uncomfortable knowledge that SAT and SIL are called by God to the same mission, and that we together constitute the body of Christ for God's mission of language development and Bible translation to the people groups we serve. This is the reality, uncomfortable as it may be. More importantly, however, we must also rest in the knowledge that no matter what happens, the Lord is in control. Ultimately, he will provide what is needed. The returns belong to the Lord, and he is ultimately responsible for them. For workers deeply invested in seeing the returns of their work, this is very uncomfortable.

Diverse ways of life and their underlying values are not the only variables in the complexities of solving a wicked multinational problem. Varied and different personalities within a team will also play a role in finding a clumsy solution and negotiating a team through it. Team members who are more introverted or shy will need quiet space and time. On the other hand, their more extroverted counterparts will desire the group to process the problem as a group. Similarly, those who wish for closure before moving on to the next issue and those who want to trust "data and facts" will struggle with the open-endedness and intuitive nature of solving a wicked problem. The leader's job is to help each teammate find interpersonal safety and security within the covenant community of the team. It is not easy, but when a team can hold each of these personality styles in appropriate tension, it can create a space for interpersonal safety and cohesion within an organization.

## "Meek" Leadership in Christ

A "meek leader" is, first of all, a person who follows Jesus, who said, "I am *meek* and lowly in heart: and ye shall find rest unto your souls"

(Matt. 11:29 KJV). Such leaders recognize a wicked problem when they encounter it. Meek leaders understand that they do not know the solution but must begin by listening and learning for a "clumsy solution." Further, meek leaders know that they cannot depend on their leadership skills and that there are no possible solutions in their leadership toolbox. Instead, they must embrace the suffering and chaos that surface when values and preferences on multinational teams collide. This is possible only when leaders commit themselves to obedience to live and lead in a manner worthy of their calling in Christ (Eph. 4:1).

Meek leaders diagnose the increasing uncertainty among their people and, in humility and steadfast trust in the Lord's guidance and provisions, resist every impulse to provide a solution for or to resolve the conflict. Instead, meek leaders, in humility, recognize the deep value conflicts among their people. Then they call their people together as members of the body of Christ—each one chosen and dearly loved—for a more in-depth discussion. This discussion leads the people into a deeper relationship with each other and with the Lord. Meek leaders understand that radical trust requires everyone to put aside elegant ideas about processes and outcomes to allow God's Holy Spirit to work. This environment is critical as the Lord speaks through the team.

Meek leaders need to recognize God's presence and instruction as the way forward. To do this, they must realize that they do not have the answer to the team's problems, and they must resist the pressure to command and control the process. Meek leaders must also recognize that alone, they cannot know the team's path. They must help their team cobble together a clumsy solution to the wicked problem. This journey is often lonely and painful, requiring obedience in Christ. "In your relationships with one another, have the same mindset as Christ Jesus: Who, being in very nature God, did not consider equality with God something to be used to his own advantage; rather, he made himself nothing by taking the very nature of a servant, being made in human likeness. And being found in appearance as a man, he humbled himself by becoming obedient to death—even death on a cross!" (Phil. 2:5–8).

Given our understanding of the complexity of cultural differences among God's people globally, our twenty-first-century commitment to "mission with" has significant unforeseen challenges. When we respond to the call of the Holy Spirit to engage in mission and to build his church, we are creating complex organizations with equally complex interpersonal relationships. Cross-cultural mission workers are prepared to make adjustments to learn a new target language and culture. But they are often surprised by the complexity and difficulty of learning the "language and culture" of their "household of faith." Many are unprepared to handle the "illogic" of their teammates' suggestions and problem-solving rationalizations.

Would you be surprised if even the heartiest of team members began to question the wisdom of working together on a multinational team? We cannot condemn those who do—those who are attracted to a more emotionally comfortable and perhaps more efficient working environment or even a greater unity of purpose. At the same time, they and we ponder, What has God intended for our ministry of "mission with" and community life?

## REFLECTION QUESTIONS

- Think about the kinds of decisions you make in ministry. What role does uncertainty play? How have you tried to manage uncertainty?
- Have you ever made a problem worse by trying to manage the uncertainty?
- Think about a recent leadership difficulty you have had. Can you identify "surprise" in that situation—false assumptions about the problem? Did uncertainty play a role?
- How have you found hope amid the chaos of cross-cultural ministry? How have you seen God's promise and preparation in your ministry context?

# 6

||||||||||||||||||||||||||||||||||||||||||||||||||||||||||||||||||||||||||||||||||||||||||||||||||||||||||||||||||

# The Deception
# of Investment Returns

## Sherwood G. Lingenfelter

My Dear Wormwood, . . . Our business is to get them away from the eternal, and from the Present. . . . It is far better to make them live in the Future. Biological necessity makes all their passions point in that direction already, so that thought about the future inflames hope and fear. Also, it is unknown to them, so that in making them think about it we make them think of unrealities. In a word, the Future is, of all things, the thing *least like* eternity. It is the most completely temporal part of time—for the Past is frozen and no longer flows, and the Present is all lit up with eternal rays. . . . Gratitude looks to the past and love to the present; fear, avarice, lust, and ambition look ahead.[1]

In this chapter, we will investigate how the language we use about future returns and the experiences we bring from living and working in the world often distract us and lead us to focus on "in the world" strategies and outcomes. While such strategies and outcomes may be good, if they undermine the work of faith and the labor of love for the mission of God, they are deceptions of our enemy.

1. Lewis, *Screwtape Letters*, 77.

## Deploying Workers in the Harvest: Two Case Studies

1. On the day Martins Atanda (author of chapter 13) sensed God's clear call, he acted quickly in obedience to that call. He left his position in the Anglican Church of Nigeria, began praying with a few whom he gathered as a board, and then launched one-week training and mobilization conferences at different locations in Nigeria. At the end of each conference, he encouraged any who were willing to join to take the next step: visit a town, talk to the leaders, listen to the people and to the Holy Spirit as they prayed for that town. Once Atanda and his emerging team had gathered information, they prayed together for direction about how to respond and to share Christ. In the power of the Spirit, they rebuked demonic, cultural, and social forces that opposed the gospel. They prayed through the night.

After his second vision in 2001, of the dark giant of Francophone (French colonial) Africa, Atanda and his team planned and executed three years of mobilization prayer tours across Francophone Africa. Since 2005, Zion World Prayer and Missions has completed targeted outreach across Francophone Africa, forming partnerships with leaders and churches in each nation and region. Working with his Nigerian team and regional and international partners, Atanda seeks to equip all whom God calls to this mission of prayer and of sharing the gospel with and showing compassion to those who have not heard.

2. Matthew Crosland's role was less apostolic and more academic. As leader of SIL's training institute in Papua New Guinea, Crosland (author of chapter 12) had the authority and responsibility for training. The challenge before him was how best to equip Melanesians called by God to plan the long and hard work of Bible translation. In order to research this challenge, Crosland had to address directly the "results-based management" model, which had become the SIL standard for managing language programs with its focus on return on investment. What Western business values undergird this model, what processes drive production, and how can the institute reframe its curriculum to equip Melanesian Christians to organize and conduct their own Bible translations?

In order to answer these questions, Crosland recruited twenty-four SIL expatriate participants from eight nations and twenty-one Melanesian participants from four regions of Papua New Guinea. Six of the Melanesian participants were fluent in English and fifteen in Tok Pisin (a language used for trade).[2] He divided his research work into phase 1—investigating the cultural values and biases of Western and Papua New Guinean Bible translators—and phase 2—conducting an experimental course (using the data collected in phase 1) to explore new options for equipping Melanesian workers. After debriefing the participants in the experimental course, Crosland and two colleagues designed a Melanesian framework for program planning and a training course to evaluate its effectiveness.

What was the point of all this hard work? After Crosland and his colleagues finished designing the new Melanesian training course, he tested it on twenty-eight Melanesian students who were to be deployed in various national-led translation programs across Papua New Guinea. "We can do this" sums up the unanimous response, and twenty-six of the twenty-eight students indicated in a survey that they were "very likely to use the Melanesian Program Planning Model." Crosland's prayer and steadfast hope is that this "model" and "training" will result in the deployment of hundreds of workers for translation to 316 language groups that do not yet have any portion of the Bible in their own language.

## Accounting for Investments

How do humans think about returns or "harvest"? Just consider how often our language about ministry mimics the language of business. For example, from mission promotional materials—maximizing our investment for outreach, a critical campaign using laser-focused online outreach tools, or online streaming educational platform for digital advertisements—all draw upon contemporary marketing strategies and language. Concepts such as investment, time, resources, talent, finance, and growth are commonly employed in our annual

2. Crosland, "Language Program Planning," 20.

ministry reviews and reports. Business language pervades the culture that we all breathe. It is like the air around us, and we are not conscious of it because we embed these concepts in language about God, sharing the gospel, partnership in ministry, reaching places, bringing hope, and expanding the harvest. This language, in itself, is not evil or necessarily inappropriate, but our language reflects our deeper cultural assumptions and priorities about work, motivation, and goals. Investments, campaigns, tools, platforms, returns, growth, outcomes, products—all are human ways to measure ourselves against some clearly defined (future) ends and to define our work to achieve those ends in ways that assert that we have done our job well. In the world of business, and often in the world of the church, these measures imply that, in comparison to others, we are better or even best.

If we examine ourselves, we see that in Western mission organizations we have also adopted the language of business management—time invested, quality assurance, cost effectiveness—to increase our productivity and to meet the demands of our mission donors. We even employ business language—investment and returns—to evaluate specific ministry effectiveness, to communicate with donors, and to promote particular ministry goals.

### Returns or Harvest?

So I pose a second question: What does Jesus say about "returns" or "harvest"? The Synoptic Gospels report five different conversations that Jesus had with the crowd and with his disciples about harvest. Matthew 9 reports the first: "When [Jesus] saw the crowds, he had compassion on them, because they were harassed and helpless, like sheep without a shepherd. Then he said to his disciples, 'The harvest is plentiful but the workers are few. Ask the Lord of the harvest, therefore, to send out workers into his harvest field'" (vv. 36–38). In this text, Jesus—the Lord of the harvest—challenges his disciples to pray for workers. He implies that these workers will be doing what he is doing: proclaiming good news and healing the sick.

In the second, longer conversation in Matthew 13, Jesus begins with the parable of the sower—or, more accurately, the parable of the soil—in which the act of sowing produces a variable harvest, utterly dependent on the soil. Later Jesus tells a second story about a sower who sows good seed, but after his work an enemy comes to sow weeds. Jesus then explains, "The one who sowed the good seed is the Son of Man. The field is the world, and the good seed stands for the people of the kingdom. The weeds are the people of the evil one, and the enemy who sows them is the devil. The harvest is the end of the age, and the harvesters are angels" (vv. 37–39). He continues, explaining that the devil will indeed enter the fields they are cultivating to plant "people of the evil one" and thus to corrupt the harvest, but God is not deceived, and the angels will sift the weeds from the good grain at God's harvest.

The remaining references in Matthew focus on the character of faithful and unfaithful servants. In Matthew 25, Jesus describes three servants, each given bags of gold by their master. Two of the servants "put the money to work," and when the master returned, they had doubled what they had been given. When the third servant returned the single bag of gold, the master rebuked him: "You wicked, lazy servant! So you knew that I harvest where I have not sown and gather where I have not scattered seed? Well then, you should have put my money on deposit with the bankers, so that when I returned I would have received it back with interest" (vv. 26–27).

What may we conclude from these parables? First, Matthew 9:38 makes it very clear that Jesus is the Lord of the harvest, the fields are ripe, and he is challenging his disciples to pray for *more workers* in that harvest. Jesus also makes the role of workers clear in the parables of the vineyard and the bags of gold—he expects them to be faithful with what they are given so that the fruits of their labor return to the Lord of the harvest.

In Mark's Gospel, Jesus further clarifies the nature of the resources and the role of the laborers: the role of the laborer is to scatter seed on the ground. Everything that follows is from God. The laborer sees the seed sprout and grow but has no comprehension or control of what happens. The soil produces grain "all by itself"—and after the harvest has come, the laborer may put his sickle to it (4:26–29). Paul concludes in 2 Corinthians 9:10, "Now he who supplies seed to the sower and bread for food will also supply and increase your store of seed and will enlarge the harvest of your righteousness."

At the beginning of this chapter, we presented case studies by Martins Atanda and Matthew Crosland describing briefly how God has moved two mission organizations to shift focus from "measuring harvest" to "mobilizing workers" for the harvest. In the pages that follow, we will examine how each organization has sought to break old habits and move toward obedience to Jesus's invitation to his disciples: "Ask the Lord of the harvest, therefore, to send out workers into his harvest field" (Matt. 9:38).

**Workers in the Harvest: Vision Shift**

The vision shift for Crosland's mission—SIL International—began in the late 1990s as leaders within SIL were evaluating more than sixty years of progress in Bible translation for the unreached. From this research they concluded that more than three thousand languages, representing three hundred million people, had no Scripture and no translation program in process. Further, the leaders looked at the New Testaments in process and completed at that time and determined that it would take between 100 and 150 years to even begin a translation program for the unreached language communities. After reading Revelation 5:1–10, John Watters, soon to be elected executive director of SIL, concluded that this lack of workers was not acceptable, and the Spirit of God moved him to work with others and propose Vision 2025—to pray and trust God that "a Bible translation project will be in progress for every people group that needs it."[3]

Turning this vision into reality required a refocus of mission—instead of counting completed New Testaments, SIL would seek to mobilize and equip global workers and count projects in progress by 2025. SIL members adopted that vision in 2000, and Crosland's case

3. Lingenfelter, *Leading Cross-Culturally*, 40.

study represents how the Papua New Guinea branch of SIL sought to implement the vision in partnership with the Bible Translation Association of Papua New Guinea.

Martins Atanda's vision shift occurred in 1995, when he was serving in his local Anglican church in Sokoto, Nigeria, and was responsible for equipping the laity for service in nearby local churches. After Atanda discovered inquiring Muslims in his local congregation, he felt the Holy Spirit lead him to resign from his position in the church and launch a program to mobilize pastors and laity to engage in evangelism and church planting to non-followers of Jesus living all around them in northern Nigeria. During this early phase, he was challenged not only to mobilize others but to lead them to share the gospel with the impoverished peoples in the surrounding cities and towns. So, instead of counting on graduates of a "school of ministry" to serve local churches, Atanda began recruiting and equipping "workers for the harvest," first in Nigeria and then in the nations.

In 2001, while Atanda was attending a World Evangelical Alliance conference in Cameroon, God gave him a vision of Francophone Africa: a giant surrounded Nigeria, in which churches and governments were bound by hypocrisy, bloodshed, and death. Atanda heard the Spirit say, "Go to these lands; teach my Word; teach people to overcome the desire for bloodshed; teach people to seek transformation; teach them business; share with them your food, clothing, shoes, and resources for well-being; pray for the ending of fighting and wars." Drawing inspiration from this vision, Atanda launched prayer tours across Francophone Africa to mobilize workers to carry the message of Jesus and actions of compassion in Jesus's name to the poor and oppressed.

As we compare these two cases, we see that both Crosland and Atanda were confronted with the magnitude of God's mission and the inadequacy of their current strategies for equipping, mobilizing, and actually accomplishing the work. For Atanda, most local church leaders and members were like the servant in Matthew 25 who buried his bag of gold in the ground. For Crosland, most SIL members in Papua New Guinea were focusing only on their own translation project and could not see any way to work differently. With the shift in vision, God raised up Atanda and Crosland to accept the leadership challenge of reinventing their task-focused training methods so as to effectively recruit and equip the next generation of workers in God's harvest.

## Persistence in Times of Uncertainty

As the Scriptures remind us, our enemy the devil is always at work seeking to distort God's Word and confound the work of faithful servants. And as Screwtape reminded us at the beginning of the chapter, one of the devil's best strategies is inducing worry about a future that we cannot control or change. Such worry about the past and the present gives us pain, regret, and a sense of failure—quenching our gratitude and love while challenging our faith and the assurance that our service will make any difference in the purpose of God.

Both Crosland and Atanda have ended their chapters on notes of uncertainty. Crosland worries about expectations (funding, accounting practices, use of time) that Melanesians find difficult or uncomfortable and worries that decisions about Melanesian projects are often made in expatriate home settings, without understanding Papua New Guinea. Atanda worries that after twenty-five years "our investment has not come to full term, has not produced the kind of fruit [churches planted, converts, growth, reproduction] among the poor, war-torn, and oppressed that we wanted."

Each man and his organization face common challenges and an uncertain future after investing so much to fulfill God's vision for their respective ministries. Table 6.1 summarizes a few of the external tests common to both ministries and their expression in very different global contexts.

The first external test is that of soil—hard, rocky, shallow, thorny, and good (Matt. 13:4–8). Atanda found that the soil in Francophone Africa was typically very hard and challenging. Unreached villagers often resisted the gospel to the point of being hostile and violent. Government leaders denied access to mission workers or set

### Table 6.1
### Persistence in Times of Testing

| External Tests | Martins Atanda Case Study | Matthew Crosland Case Study |
| --- | --- | --- |
| Soil | Resistant people groups | Receptivity to translation |
| No rain | Seeds that don't sprout | Returns-based donors |
| Slow growth | Seeds that are slow to grow | Melanesian cyclical time |
| Satan's deception | Weeds among recruits | Weeds among recruits |

conditions so difficult that people feared to respond. Church people expressed despair and members ceased to witness, fearing the heat and thorns of a religious tradition that was binding the poor and helpless around them.

Crosland encountered shallow soil, thorny soil, and good soil. While a significant number of Papua New Guineans have responded to Christianity, most of them have never imagined the possibility of Scripture in their own language. Further, very few have been educated to a level to comprehend what Bible translation is and how it might benefit their people. Less than a third of church leaders have mastered English, and the more successful tribal groups have relied on the Tok Pisin translation of the Bible.

The second issue is no rain to water the seed. In North Africa, drought and desert are the primary causes of poverty and oppression, and spiritual drought is the norm for the very few who hear and receive the gospel. In this kind of environment, seeds of the gospel do not sprout, and even when they do sprout, the soil is so hard and the resistance so great that those touched often fall away.

For Crosland and Bible translation in Papua New Guinea, the drought is about funding. Most of the educated people in Papua New Guinea, if given the opportunity, will find work that provides an hourly or weekly wage. While a few might volunteer their time to work on translation, for most, some compensation is essential so that they can feed their families. However, people in the West who are motivated to donate toward such translation projects typically look for predictable and easily quantifiable returns on their investment. They indeed have asked for "returns-based" reports and products as a condition for their gifts. This is challenging for Melanesians, who see productivity through a very different cultural lens.

The third issue is slow growth. In North Africa, the seeds of faith and response to the gospel seem incredibly slow to germinate. Atanda details in chapter 13 how, after twenty-five years of working, the "harvest" consists of only a few churches scattered across a vast area. And while there are places where the seeds seem to be sprouting, the intense heat of opposition often causes these sprouts to grow very slowly or even wither away.

The problem for Western translators and donors in Papua New Guinea is cyclical time: the agricultural calendar of Melanesians. Westerners like to have things on a linear calendar, and they insist on funding based on annual reports. As Crosland documents in chapter 12, Melanesians do not think or work in this particular way. Thus, growth among Melanesians may occur in spurts and may be related to the pressures of the local community, illnesses, and opposition that are not part of the program but are rather part of a cycle of life that makes some time periods more profitable than others.

Finally, both regions are subject to the enemy—the devil, as reported in Matthew 13. Atanda relates how a few of his evangelists to an unreached group "disappeared into thin air." He also reports how some participants claimed to be committed to mission, while in reality they were seeking their own ends. Only the Lord knows the hearts of these men and women and knows which are committed to his purpose and which are agents of the enemy.

In Papua New Guinea, the challenges are similar. Participants may look at Bible translation as an opportunity for income and may go through the training with hidden career and economic motives rather than as workers for the mission of God. Time spent training such men and women is wasted if, after a time, they walk away. Further, the funding that is available for Bible translation cannot compete with the wages often available from jobs in secular arenas, with the consequence that some workers—participating with wrong motives—leave in the midst of project work.

Both Crosland's and Atanda's organizations are deeply committed to equipping workers for the harvest. But Satan is always seeking to sow weeds among those God calls and to undermine their work in ways that will cause donors and supporters to lose heart. For these reasons alone, we must not neglect the spiritual disciplines of prayer, the work of faith, and the labor of love. Without these, we are helpless to counter the enemy: "Think of the various tests you encounter as occasions for joy. After all, you know that the testing of your faith produces endurance. Let this endurance complete its work so that you may be fully mature, complete, and lacking in nothing" (James 1:2–4 CEB).

## In-Christ Responses to the "Returns" Deception

> Gratitude looks to the past and love to the present; fear, avarice, lust, and ambition look ahead.[4]

The temptation to focus our ministry on measurable future returns is a deception of our enemy. Jesus is clearly Lord of the harvest, and we have no control over the process. In his final instructions to his disciples in the Gospel of John, Jesus reinforces my conclusion. The whole process of our work for his mission is utterly dependent on our relationship with him: "Remain in me, as I also remain in you. No branch can bear fruit by itself; it must remain in the vine. Neither can you bear fruit unless you remain in me. 'I am the vine; you are the branches. If you remain in me and I in you, you will bear much fruit; apart from me you can do nothing'" (John 15:4–5). If we want to be productive servants, it is possible only when we "remain in the vine." All our efforts apart from the vine are useless, and everything else—soil, rain, sprouting, growing, ripening, and harvest—is in his control.

So what shall we conclude about our language and default habits of assessing the returns of our performance? The Scriptures suggest that if we seek to motivate and justify by our returns rather than by our obedience, we will always be disappointed. God has simply asked us to obey him and to follow Jesus in our service and unity with others.

4. Lewis, *Screwtape Letters*, 77.

It is only when we are connected to the vine that we may bear fruit, and it is the vine that produces the fruit, not the branches. When we look at how Jesus assesses our performance in Matthew 25:31–40, it has nothing to do with the number of converts, the number of people fed, or the number of prisoners released. It has everything to do with what flows from our hearts.

## REFLECTION QUESTIONS

- To what extent does your mission use business language to measure organizational and personal performance?
- What do you find in Scripture that may challenge this practice, and what do you find that may support it? Make a list of texts and compare them.
- What does Jesus teach us to look for when he sends us out two by two?
- What does your church teach you to look for when it sends you out?

# 7

‖‖‖‖‖‖‖‖‖‖‖‖‖‖‖‖‖‖‖‖‖‖‖‖‖‖‖‖‖‖‖‖‖‖‖‖‖‖‖‖‖‖‖‖‖‖‖‖‖‖‖‖‖‖‖‖‖‖‖‖‖‖‖‖‖‖‖‖‖‖‖‖‖‖‖‖‖‖‖‖‖‖‖‖‖‖‖

# Can You Disagree?
# Can You Work Together?

SHERWOOD G. LINGENFELTER

My Dear Wormwood, . . . This, indeed, is probably one of the Enemy's motives for creating a dangerous world—a world in which moral issues really come to the point. He sees as well as you do that courage is not simply *one* of the virtues, but the form of every virtue at the testing point, which means, at the point of highest reality. A chastity, or honesty, or mercy, which yields to danger will be chaste or honest or merciful only on conditions. Pilate was merciful till it became risky.[1]

The guiding question of this chapter is this: Can you disagree and yet work together? Leading a team to consciously identify aspects of a problem upon which they agree and then to bring to the surface issues upon which they disagree is as important as defining what they collectively want. The disagreements will usually emerge from danger—feelings of risk, inhibition, or potential loss that members may harbor personally or collectively. No matter how virtuous people

---

1. Lewis, *Screwtape Letters*, 148.

may be, danger always undermines virtue. This chapter examines and compares how two leaders of two very different multinational teams faced the challenge of danger—hidden values and fears—undermining the virtue of trust and empowerment among the members of each household of faith to accomplish its mission. Each leader faced four difficult tasks:

1. To surface hidden values and fears among team members.
2. To bridge these value gaps and fears "in Christ."
3. To surface default habits of working and decision-making.
4. To construct processes that enable team members to work together in unity.

### Different Leaders, Values, Processes: Two "Households of Faith"

1. The SIM Ghana leadership team led by Penny Bakewell (author of chapter 10) was composed of eight members with four different nationalities and diverse personalities. The Brits and Canadians had much in common culturally, but brought many differences in personality and preferences for participation. The Korean and North East Indians on the team brought deep respect for hierarchy and the authority of the team leader. Many members suffered from anxiety about self and fear of offending others on the team. The Western extroverts tended to dominate the meetings, and the others feared to challenge them or even to present different viewpoints. Further, the Asians had quite different values and expectations about leader-follower interactions on a team.

When Bakewell accepted the team leadership role for SIM Ghana, she recognized immediately that the challenges of this work were beyond her depth of experience and knowledge. She acknowledged that she had neither the experience nor the skills to lead such a group. Her first challenge was to "get to know team members" in such a way that "you know you know." She understood that once she knew her team well, she could then ask questions—publicly or privately—to reveal the values in play that were contributing to her wicked problem.

2. Matthew Crosland (author of chapter 12) had in effect two teams: (1) members of SIL International from the United States, Australia, Britain, and other nations and (2) Melanesian team members from diverse linguistic and tribal backgrounds in Papua New Guinea. While the numbers of people involved in both teams were approximately the same, Crosland clearly had two clusters—highly educated expatriates from SIL and tribal participants who had been trained locally for translation work in their respective mother tongues. Anxiety in these groups centered on radically different cultures of origin and an agreement among the Melanesians that they were the inferior, younger, and dependent brothers in the partnership. The SIL-affiliated expatriates feared the loss of their way of work and their significance as "properly trained" Bible translators.

Crosland had extensive experience with both SIL and Melanesian translators, yet he was not trained as a translator or engaged in translation work. As director of the institute for training Papua New Guinean nationals to do translation, he served as the "bridge" leader between unequal partners, half of whom served with an "equality" myth of operation. Crosland had worked with all the people on this team for several years, and he knew them well. His challenge was to learn how to bridge the huge cultural divide he had experienced in his role as director for the training of Melanesian leaders and mother-tongue translators.

## "Creating a Reflective Space" for Listening and Learning

Bakewell and Crosland both pondered how they could and should act as God's servant to their teams. Both leaders reached the conclusion that their role in Christ was to bring team members into a "reflective space" from which to begin to process the challenges before each team. By engaging team members in such a way to surface and acknowledge their anxieties and fears of loss, they also were creating an opportunity for the team to submit these fears to Christ, collectively seek the guidance of the Holy Spirit, and individually be about the work of faith and the labor of love as members of one body.

Fortunately, SIM International understood Bakewell's dilemma and invited her to join a leadership development cohort with seven other new directors in September 2018. As part of the process, the participants reflected together on the vision and core values statements of SIM and on the question "What do we believe?" Bakewell realized that these SIM documents gave her legitimate authority to lead her team to reflect upon these core values. She understood that SIM's stated mission was "to make disciples of the Lord Jesus Christ in communities where He is least known."[2] She concluded that everyone in Christ is equally valued and valuable for this mission and that the formation of members into a multinational team was critical for SIM's purpose. She pondered the biblical images of leadership—shepherd, servant, steward—that defined the core metaphors for SIM leadership practice.[3]

When Bakewell returned to Ghana in 2018, pondering her team challenge, she went back to the Scriptures for help and was deeply moved by John 10:14–15, in which Jesus declares, "I am the good shepherd; I know my sheep and my sheep know me—just as the Father knows me and I know the Father—and I lay down my life for the sheep." Reflecting on this text, she realized that the biggest challenge before her was to know her people as Jesus knows his sheep. She understood the value of diversity, which brought many skills, diverse knowledge, and creativity to the members of SIM teams.

Crosland faced a very different challenge. As a member of SIL in charge of training for Melanesian nationals, he prayerfully understood his role—"steward and servant in Christ"—to mean representing the "senior" partner, SIL, and acting as the leadership bridge to the "junior" (but, in Christ, equal) Melanesian partners. He had been thoroughly trained in the mission and vision of SIL, including the results-based approach to translation. After years of work and relationship with Melanesian nationals in the training institute, he recognized the radical differences between Western and Melanesian cultures and struggled to find a way to discuss these differences and

2. "Our Mission," SIM Australia, https://www.sim.org.au/About/Our-Mission.
3. Bremner, *Images of Leadership*.

draw people together around their shared vision to bring Scripture to 316 language groups in Papua New Guinea. He knew that SIL's goals could not be accomplished without a radical shift in SIL's training culture toward a more "people focused" training, and he depended on the Holy Spirit to guide him as he sought to create a reflective space to make room for this shift.

### What Hinders, What Helps? Research (Labor of Love)

What are some practical strategies we may employ to lead team members to engage hidden values and fears and to collaborate toward an in-Christ resolution of such fears for Christ's mission? Given their personal history with their respective team members, Bakewell and Crosland adopted very different strategies to research, analyze, and resolve this problem. Though Bakewell knew her team members well, when she became director, she found she was ignorant about how they liked to be led and what conditions would bring out the best in each member. She began the hard work of deepening her relationship with each of them through personal conversations and semistructured interviews.

Crosland, who had a much longer personal history with his SIL and Papua New Guinea teammates, designed a research project that would enable these unequal partners to gain a much deeper understanding of their cultural preferences and default habits for the very serious work of training tribal people to translate Scripture. We will briefly review Bakewell's and Crosland's respective research strategies and findings to illustrate the complexity of doing the labor of love with members of complex multinational teams.

The first step in our comparison is to examine the nature of the two leaders' wicked problems. Very early, Bakewell discovered that silence was a common problem in meetings. Her experience supported research that found that typically 60 percent of the participant contributions came from two very vocal people. Crosland describes his wicked problem as an SIL older brother, PNG (Papua New Guinea) younger brother challenge (see p. 135), with a large power gap between the two and the locus of control residing in the elder brother: the younger "submits" to the elder. The cultural differences between the SIL and Melanesian partners were great enough that neither could conceive of how to manage these differences.

Bakewell and Crosland each designed research plans to address these issues. Bakewell asked, "What helps and what hinders?" To answer her questions, she began a series of conversations with couples and individual team members that provided an opportunity for these individuals to seek within themselves an understanding of their personal values and fears. These conversations were clearly a labor of love: Where can we safely meet, how do I begin each conversation, how do I ensure that each person feels respected and honored, how much time do we need together to process these questions, how do I reflect back what I have learned about them, and do I have permission to discuss this with others? As people responded, Bakewell gently nudged her team members to examine and explain their motives and values so they might understand and engage more freely with each other in the process.

Crosland designed a research plan to reveal value differences between the "older siblings" and the "younger siblings" on his team. To achieve this, he created three card sorts—three sets of five cards—picturing five alternative values on the topics of (1) production vs. relationships, (2) linear vs. cyclical time orientation, and (3) analytic vs. holistic thinking. He asked participants to order the cards from most important to least important and to explain why they picked that order. He also designed four vignettes: open-ended stories in the local cultural context that put the subject of the story into a difficult situation and did not offer a resolution. Working with a sample of ten expatriates and ten nationals, he administered the card sorts, the vignettes, and a follow-up interview in one sitting with each participant, recording each interview. This was clearly a labor of love for him and stimulated reciprocity from the participants.

After Crosland finished processing all the data he had collected, he presented it to the mixed group of participants working on the Melanesian program planning project. They were all surprised at the value contrasts that surfaced between them, and they noticed how the responses of the expatriates clustered around one set of values and those of the nationals clustered around another set. Once they had processed and understood these wide differences, they gained respect for the "other" and were more willing to consider change.

Through their respective research, Bakewell and Crosland each gained a much deeper understanding both of the values of individual team members and of how these values clustered within their teams. They analyzed their data to discover the factors so crucial to leading their teams to more effectively engage their wicked problem.

As Bakewell processed her information, she observed that leadership team members from the UK and Canada shared much in common, but also showed important differences concerning what hindered them from contributing to team meetings or helped them to contribute. She also observed that the North East Indians and Korean on the team shared similar values about both teamwork and process, yet had some very different emotions, expectations, and anxieties about the process. Culturally, some members of the team needed permission to talk, while others insisted on freedom. Personalities varied such that some needed time and help to prepare for discussions, while others thrived when talking through issues on the spot. The use of English as a lingua franca inhibited members' contributions in some significant ways, requiring mutual concessions on everyone's part. As Bakewell dug deeper, she found Erin Meyer's book *The Culture Map* helpful for understanding cultural and personality differences.

Crosland's research confirmed for him—and convinced his team members—that SIL's linear time orientation, analytical thinking, and production orientation were critical factors—contrasting with Melanesian values—that inhibited national workers from learning and working effectively in their local contexts. SIL members feared that the loss of these distinctives would undermine the progress, credibility, and completion of translations. It was this research that led the team members to work creatively toward a new training model for national workers.

Why would Bakewell and Crosland do this hard work of research? As we reflect on their stories, we see that both had a personal vision and a commitment to their team members that motivated them to undertake this labor of love. As team leaders, they each believed that by working together, patiently listening, learning, and sharing with one another, their teams would be more effective in fulfilling their mission as servants of the Lord Jesus Christ and of one another.

### Persistence and Hope—Leading "in Christ" for Change

What are some practical strategies we can use to help team members bring to the surface their feelings of danger and break default process habits—customary routines—of work and decision-making? In the Bakewell and Crosland case studies, we see three similar strategies both leaders used: (1) preplanned engagement, (2) collaborative processing of next steps on the basis of shared values, and (3) engaging members to define together structural change and new processes. Both leaders had a personal vision to create a structure and a process that could bridge the high risk value and process the gaps inherent in their team cultures and history.

### A "Bridge" Organization: Crosland

Crosland, appreciating the almost rigid commitment of SIL to results-based management of language programs, invested months of energy and planning before he attempted to lead his team toward change. He invited Barry Borneman, an Australian outsider, to teach a people-focused one-week program planning course to the Melanesian members of his team. Borneman, drawing from his experience with Australian Aborigines, used "people orientation" to teach the old results-based course, commonly used in SIL Australia and SIL-PNG. Crosland then collected evaluations from his team members and spent the next week debriefing and brainstorming with them—both the SIL and the Melanesian members—about how to redesign the standard program planning model used in the course. During this time of reflection, Crosland led the team in evaluating the course design with reference to his data—priorities for time, process, and relationship—in the analysis of the card sorts, vignettes, and interview research. By the time this work was completed, both groups were at peace with one another and with the process.

In the end, Crosland's team created a new model for a Melanesian program planning course, and while it had many of the same features as the SIL results-based management course—indicating stewardship of the past—the core value features had shifted dramatically to serve God's mission for the future. The team of SIL expatriates and Melanesians collaborated to redefine core concepts, replacing "inputs" and "outputs" with "planning" and "resources." In addition, the Melanesian planning model gave priority to vision and community discussion. The most radical change was the move from linear time to "seasonal cycles" of activity—paralleling the agricultural life of the Melanesian people—in which mother-tongue translators could do their work.

## "Mission with" Leadership: Bakewell

Bakewell, facing the recurring challenge of leadership team meetings governed by "silence," concluded that premeeting preparation was vital to encourage second-language workers to participate. Meeting with these workers beforehand, bringing their fears to the surface, and assuring them that they would be asked for their ideas helped them to prepare. Bakewell then invited the team to gather and make a list of guiding principles to which all members affirmed their commitment: all are equal in Christ, all opinions are valued, all are led by the Spirit, diversity leads to richness and creativity. The team decided to read together these guiding principles before each meeting.

Finally, Bakewell asked her team members to make some commitments to support changes in meeting structure and processes. The first was a commitment to openness: share freely, encourage open discussion, seek clarification, and ensure that everyone has understood. The second was a commitment to more effective communication processes: speak slowly, use the whiteboard to record, observe body language, summarize frequently, and welcome silence as space to think. The third was a commitment to valuing one another in that process: affirm every contribution, give teammates the opportunity to explain, ask the quiet ones to speak, allow "I have nothing to add" responses. The final commitment was to make the meeting a time of trust, love, and friendship by listening well (without interruption), allowing informal discussion, and being thankful as team members seeking God's will together.

Throughout this process, Bakewell viewed herself as a servant and shepherd of her team. Working from these commitments, she guided team members in ways intended to alleviate their anxieties, to bridge the differences of culture and personality among them, and to help them work more effectively together for their shared vision of bringing the gospel to the unreached in Ghana.

### Can You Disagree? Can You Work Together?
### Persistence and Hope

> A chastity, or honesty, or mercy, which yields to danger will be chaste or honest or merciful only on conditions. Pilate was merciful till it became risky.[4]

From the comparative analysis of these two case studies, it is clear that multinational teamwork is often derailed by the personal risks of anxiety about self, fear of offending others, inhibitions of cultural identity, and fear of losing that which we deem good or best in our work or ministry. Bakewell and Crosland asked their teams two critical questions: Can you disagree? And, when you do disagree, is it possible to bridge these disagreements and work together? We see in their case studies that the work of faith involves deep reflection—including confession to overcome fear and repentance to restore trust—both by leaders and by team members if we are to bridge the fear and mistrust, fueled by our personal and cultural differences, that we bring with us to ministry. The outcome of this work is not assured, by any means, but both Bakewell and Crosland have persisted in the work of faith and the labor of love. They live in hope that those who follow tomorrow will—in Christ—continue their work.

4. Lewis, *Screwtape Letters*, 148.

We have also seen that there is no single solution to resolve these issues. Bakewell and Crosland adopted very different research strategies to bring deep anxiety issues to the surface and then devoted much labor of love to lead their team members toward resolution. Crosland called this process a "clumsy compromise," which in his case *replaced* what most SIL members believed was the right and elegant solution to program planning. Bakewell and Crosland each led their teams to a place where they were willing to slow down, listen, and speak in ways that valued one another. And, in both cases, that work of faith in Christ led to mutual acceptance among team members—in spite of the risks involved—and to validation of the larger vision of their respective organizations and hope for the years of ministry ahead.

## REFLECTION ACTIVITIES

- If your team is polarized, consider asking team members to "argue" for the other side.
- Invite team members to write or tell a story that describes the problem and what implementing the solution would look and feel like.
- Invite visually oriented members to draw a picture of what an outcome might look like.
- Role-play a drama enacting what a potential solution might look like if it were implemented.

# 8

# Tensions between
# Personal Identity and Role

SHERWOOD G. LINGENFELTER

No one who is tested should say, "God is tempting me!" This is because God is not tempted by any form of evil, nor does he tempt anyone. Everyone is tempted by their own cravings; they are lured away and enticed by them. Once those cravings conceive, they give birth to sin; and when sin grows up, it gives birth to death. (James 1:13–15 CEB)

But I am afraid that just as Eve was deceived by the serpent's cunning, your minds may somehow be led astray from your sincere and pure devotion to Christ. (2 Cor. 11:3)

This chapter focuses on exploring the tensions between personal identity, role, and in-Christ relationships within multinational teams. In chapter 4, Julie reminded us that uncertainty about authority is a critical factor undermining teamwork. If we dig deeper, we will discover that such uncertainty flows from two very common desires or hungers prevalent in the world of secular and government leadership. These two hungers are

- "to have an effect, . . . to contribute, . . . to make a positive difference," and
- "for authority that will provide orientation and reassurance in times of stress and fear."[1]

While these desires seem positive at first glance, when others oppose, our desire has the potential to overpower us emotionally and precipitate actions that may become destructive to unity. The first—to have an effect, to contribute—threatens when we are *certain* our personal action is essential to accomplish something we deem *significant*. The second—"for authority that will provide orientation and reassurance"—surfaces most profoundly when we are in crisis, when value conflicts come into play and we feel the need for *authority to control* things so they will turn out "right."

## To Control or to Make a Positive Difference?

In my 2012–2017 research on leaders in situations of crisis,[2] I discovered that leaders who did not understand their hungers to control and to make a positive difference were blinded by them—unable to explore alternatives for change in times of crisis. They consistently defaulted to the use of authority and power or to the compelling demands of the particular goal they had in mind, driven by their hunger for significance. Further, since they were not able to manage their own hungers for meaning and authority, they were ineffective in guiding others whose values and hungers were in conflict with theirs.

Human hungers for significance and authority are so normal that we rarely think about them. Such hungers often lead church and mission leaders to accomplish many positive things. Most people aspire to do something significant, and most want and need the affirmation

---

1. Parks, *Leadership Can Be Taught*, 2.
2. Lingenfelter, *Leadership in the Way of the Cross*, 30–39.

and acceptance of others. Most people who respond to God's calling to mission do so believing that obedience will lead to significant meaning and purpose in their lives. We also hunger for the authority that will enable us to achieve our meaning and purpose.

My point is that human hungers are normal and common and may potentially contribute much that is good to our team mission. However, the problem with such hungers is that all are tempted by them, and, when left unchecked, "they are lured away and enticed by them. Once those cravings conceive, they give birth to sin; and when sin grows up, it gives birth to death" (James 1:14–15 CEB).

In Julie's case (described in chap. 4), it was clear that the members of her language development team had very different views and "hungers" regarding how to organize their programs. When they were asked to embrace a collaborative team strategy for this work, the ensuing crisis and value conflict led at least two members of the group to take authority for their own projects rather than cooperate with the others. Facing the stress of figuring out how to move forward, those two asserted their authority to go it alone in order to achieve personal goals for language development and translation.

In the two cases for comparison in this chapter, we will see the authors struggling with team members to answer two important questions: Why am I here? and What does it mean to be a team? The first question is about significance and meaning. The second is about how we exercise authority and control in relationship to one another.

## Why Am I Here? Two Case Studies—Identity and Significance

Robert and Elizabeth McLean (authors of chap. 11) are responsible for training that equips men and women for long-term ministry with Global Pentecostal Mission (GPM)[3] in Central Asia. Their program, which lasts one to three years, focuses on language learning, cultural understanding, and practical knowledge and skills for communicating the gospel, discipling new believers, and assisting local churches. Over

3. Global Pentecostal Mission (GPM) is a pseudonym, used here to protect the identity of the organization.

a period of seven years, the McLeans have served growing numbers of new members and veteran recruits of GPM from North America, Latin America, and Europe. They have found it strategically useful to distribute their new recruits into smaller satellite teams in which members can build community as well as language, culture, and ministry skills. Within these satellite teams, they have designated one person or couple as team leader—to guide team-related activities—and the others have had supporting roles for the training and ministry experiences.

The McLeans found that team members in training struggle with different conceptions of authority: hierarchy vs. equality. Often, the issue of "who is team leader" led to stress among those not chosen; some felt diminished, others relieved, others insulted. Latin American and European team members varied in both their cultural and their personal expectations and viewed their American leaders with some skepticism. Probably most of these trainees at some time imagined themselves becoming a team leader. Further, those who were not team leaders in satellite teams struggled to understand their status and contribution. Position within the team, status, and contribution were important issues for team members, affected by varying cultural expectations and personalities.

However, for many, the more important question concerned "personal meaning" in their team assignment: Is my contribution essential? The McLeans' diverse recruits frequently expressed concerns in the first person, referring to "my" preferences, "my" decisions, "my" experience, and the needs of "my" family. They gave priority to "personal agency" over team thinking and decision-making.

Penny Bakewell of SIM Ghana (see chaps. 7 and 10) had a very different challenge. Her new leadership role involved gathering ministry leaders scattered across Ghana to form a leadership team and to engage them to collaborate in planning strategic work for the nation, coordinating all SIM local ministry teams. The Korean and North East Indian ministry leaders—members of her leadership team—clearly saw themselves in subordinate positions under Bakewell and understood their role and meaning with reference to those positions. The British, Canadian, and American members blended home cultures of hierarchy and equality in different ways and tended to see their roles as partners with Bakewell as having varied status within the leadership team with reference to their individual skills and experiences. For these Westerners, role was more about skill and contribution than about hierarchy.

For Bakewell, the challenge was getting members to participate in meaningful ways that respected and honored the contributions of each. The personalities of the team members played an important role in their interactions, as did their cultures of origin. Distinct personality traits surfaced as she listened to and learned from them—one said "I think out loud," another said "I need preparation," and a third said "I worry about offending." The members were making decisions about participation on the basis of their own emotional state and feelings of security or insecurity about how the team should work. And each was inhibited in some way by a sense of personal security and agency.

So the question "Why am I here?" frames the issues of role, meaning, and significance for each team member in both case studies. In both case studies, team members struggled with different feelings about hierarchy and equity. The question "Why am I here?" is really about symbols: title, role, and meaning. What role am I to play and what meaning will I gain from my participation? Behind these questions is an assumption that "my agency must be significant." In both case studies, these questions were an important part of the dynamics of the team relationship.

In each case, team members struggled with their leader's expectations that they would create a collaborative community of spiritual formation and action. On the Central Asian teams, members took defensive postures—"my calling" for ministry and leadership and "this is the way we do it in our churches" ministry. Many resisted the "collaborative ideal" of teamwork presented by the leaders and defaulted to their individual preferences. The SIM Ghana leaders gave passive resistance—silence—to Bakewell in her team meetings, defaulting to preministry cultural patterns of direct or indirect confrontation, submission in silence to one's leader, and speaking or guarding one's "mind." Fearing personal loss of meaning and acceptance (and for

Asians, potential loss of face), members resisted Bakewell's ideal of collaboration and full participation with silence.

So we see in these two cases that members' questions about personal significance become a "wicked problem" with hidden implications for the individuals' ability to work together effectively on a team. When members focus on their "role" and "personal meaning" in a group, they evaluate matters in very personal ways so that the risk of losing what seems critical to one's meaning and purpose provokes caution and reluctance to work together within a "foreign" community.

## What Does It Mean to Be a Team? Identity and Authority

Andy Crouch, in his recent book *Strong and Weak*,[4] argues that "in Christ," authority and vulnerability must always be understood as interdependent realities. Jesus declares, "All authority in heaven and on earth has been given to me" (Matt. 28:18) and "the Son of Man did not come to be served, but to serve, and to give his life as a ransom for many" (20:28). Working from this perspective, Crouch defines *authority* as "a shared reality embedded in the roles and power given to us by the people that we serve" and *vulnerability* as the "exposure to meaningful risk"[5] that is inherent in the exercise of that authority in our service to God and to God's people.

The diversity of participants in these two case studies provides significant challenges for team leaders. We see their aversion to "risk" in many contexts. People coming from four or more nations probably have at least four different understandings of authority as a "shared reality embedded in the roles and power given to us by the people that we serve." Our intent here is not to examine the characteristics of that diversity, since Geert Hofstede and Erin Meyer have done that well.[6] Rather, we will examine how the challenges of these different

---

4. Crouch, *Strong and Weak*, 4.

5. *Vulnerability*, for Crouch, is always "exposure to meaningful risk" rather than "emotional transparency," which is the more common definition. See *Strong and Weak*, 29–32.

6. Hofstede et al., *Cultures and Organizations*; Meyer, *Culture Map*.

perspectives make it so difficult to define the meaning of *team* and *teamwork*—thus creating a wicked problem.

We begin with a question: Who defines this "shared reality"? It is clear in the McLean case study that, in the world, Robert and Elizabeth McLean have been given their roles and responsibility for equipping recruits by their sponsoring organization, GPM. But they have learned by the pain of experience that if no one is following, one is not leading. Further, unless they work with the recruits they serve and earn their respect and trust, the authority from GPM is powerless. They, the leaders, have recognized that all spiritual authority is in Christ and that they must choose the pathway of "vulnerability in Christ" to win this trust.

Many GPM recruits in Central Asia resisted "working for" Americans and resisted their notion of "getting on board" in teamwork. When these recruits were assigned to satellite teams in order to gain practical experience of teamwork and ministry together, they often rejected each other, asserting their experience and freedom to do what they had done in the past. And when the McLeans confronted them—asking can you adjust, will you submit, are you willing to belong—some resisted their efforts while others supported them. This process was and continues to be tested again and again.

In the case of SIM Ghana, SIM International appointed Bakewell as Ghana director from among her peers, many of whom she had worked alongside and others of whom were new to the nation and the team. Bakewell too faced the challenge of converting her institutional authority into a "shared reality . . . given to us by the people that we serve."[7] She had both seasoned and new recruits on her team, and all of them brought different cultures of participation with them. All understood that Bakewell was director, but what this role meant to each of them varied. Further, all interpreted authority and its application to their ministry on the basis of their home context, so they responded to her on the basis of past experience.

In contrast to GPM teams, which typically chose to resist American authority, Bakewell's team members expressed concerns about "my

7. Crouch, *Strong and Weak*, 49.

role and my fears" and about "how and where do I fit?" Unwilling to take the risk of surrendering what they knew from their home context, they chose silence as a risk-free option. These internal questions about authority and blending cultures had to be resolved before they could grasp the meaning of being a team. Bakewell's commitment to "know my people" won their trust, and they then empowered her to define with them ways they might collaborate, make decisions, and act as a team across their cultural barriers.

## What I Am in Christ: Meek, Gentle, Humble

Throughout this book, we have asked how one can be "in the world" but not "of the world" because of our new identity as adopted siblings in Christ. Authority and significance in Christ reflect, at the core, radical differences from parallel concepts in the Greco-Roman world, which was characterized by competition and domination among men and women to gain position and maintain honor in their respective spheres of influence.[8] When we are in Christ, we experience a radical change of heart; in the Gospel of Matthew, Jesus actually describes his heart when he says, "I am gentle [meek] and humble in heart" (11:29). The Greek word for "meek" (*praus*) in this text was sometimes used to describe a horse in harness.[9] This connotation is critical for application to the leadership of teams—a leader has power but is in harness to Christ. Jaime Sanchez of Biola University notes how Jesus uses the metaphor of a yoke to explain the use of *meek* in Matthew 11:30:

> [Jesus] then states succinctly, "for my yoke is easy and my burden is light" (Matt. 11:30, NIV). Most English translations . . . use the word "easy" to describe the yoke. Yet, the same word is translated elsewhere in the New Testament as "kind." For example, "Be kind to one another" (Eph. 4:32) and "you have tasted the kindness of the

8. Russell, *In the World but Not of the World*, 160.
9. In early modern English, horse handlers talked about "meeking a horse," or getting it under control.

Lord" (1 Pet. 2:3). So, . . . [this] verse could also be translated "For my yoke is kind."[10]

So if we understand *authority* as meaning a shared reality embedded in the roles and power given to us by the people we serve and exercised in Christ, we then lead and serve out of gentle and humble hearts—"power in harness"—and under his yoke of kindness.

## What I Am Not in Christ: Title, Structure, Role

Authority in Christ is always based on the presence and power of God, as is best evidenced in the life and ministry of the apostle Paul.[11] In his letters to communities of faith across the Roman Empire, the apostle Paul makes very clear how his leadership is different from the structures of the world. First, his authority is experiential, flowing out of his life testimony rather than from a title, structure, or role. In his first Letter to the Thessalonians, Paul models transformation, stating clearly how he is not of the world.

- He is not a charlatan—impure, cunning—but rather faithful to a trust (2:3–5).
- He uses not flattery but gentleness and love (2:5–8).
- He embodies the message, like a father (2:9–12).[12]

In his second Letter to the Corinthians, Paul takes the posture of weakness (jars of clay) and suffering (crushed, perplexed, struck down), rejecting wholly the Corinthian postures of competition, rivalry, and power (4:7–5:10). Relying entirely on the "all-surpassing power . . . from God" (4:7), Paul embodies an ethos of suffering with Christ.[13]

Paul consistently demonstrates the work of the Holy Spirit in his life. It is out of his *living in the Spirit* that he is given power from

10. Jaime Sanchez, "The Messiah as Care-Giver," 2020 Advent Project (Biola University), December 16, 2020, http://ccca.biola.edu/advent/2020/#day-dec-16.

11. Russell, *In the World but Not of the World*, 161.

12. Thompson, *Apostle of Persuasion*, 85–86.

13. Thompson, *Apostle of Persuasion*, 99.

God, and then he is given *authority* in the communities he serves *by those people he is serving*. He declares that the love of Christ compels us (2 Cor. 5:14; cf. Gal. 2:20) and that since "one died for all, and therefore all died," then "those who live should no longer live for themselves but for him who died for them" (2 Cor. 5:14–15). When he admonishes the Corinthians to "follow my example, as I follow the example of Christ" (1 Cor. 11:1), he earns their trust by obedience to Christ.

### Shepherd, Servant: Knowing and Submitting

As we reflect on the SIM team in Ghana and the GPM teams in Central Asia, we see that Bakewell and the McLeans exemplify the practice of "authority in Christ" for cross-cultural teamwork. Bakewell began with a clear understanding that Jesus defined the way: "I am the good shepherd; I know my sheep and my sheep know me" (John 10:14). She diligently set about the work of "knowing" the members of her team. She persisted in "knowing" until members gave everyone room to speak in team meetings. She watched as the Spirit at work among them overcame the silence that had burdened their team meetings.

The McLeans followed Paul's example to the Thessalonians, being "at home" together with multiple team members and sharing lives during the two years of training. They engaged in the work of faith together, praying together, sharing their zeal for the gospel, and working together with their team members in the action of ministry. They shared their financial resources and understood that a team is not about maintaining "equality" but rather about mutual gifts and submitting to one another in Christ.

In times of crisis and even rejection, the McLeans persisted in hope, waiting patiently for the Spirit to soften those who were hard and forgiving again and again until the Spirit led these struggling members to follow. They lived and served in hope, knowing that some would resist and leave, but—until then—forgiving, loving, and waiting until God did the work of "new creation" in a troubled couple or team.

## Servant, Shepherd: Learning and Vulnerable

The hunger for significance among team members surfaced repeatedly in the stories and interviews in both of these case studies, but these team leaders took the risk of empowering others and allowing the Holy Spirit to do the work of grace among their team members. Bakewell stepped out of her role as director and into the role of shepherd. She then did the work of a shepherd, investing her time and energy into getting to know her team members intimately. By submitting to them and serving them, she led them to submit to one another. By taking on the low status of "learner," she built the trust essential to serve as their leader.

The McLeans redefined their title and role from "directors of training" to servants and shepherds. Robert McLean preaches to all teams monthly from a place of vulnerability and hope—exposing his weaknesses even if, as a leader, it creates culturally awkward moments—and proclaiming his reliance upon God. The McLeans together share what they have, love generously, and repent and forgive even when it hurts. They believe deeply that "team" is an example of the family of God in action, and they serve others with hope that members will serve one another. They know that the values of the kingdom of God *can* have an impact on team life, structures, and leadership styles.

They live these values with these teams. When another couple has a passion to work in a high-risk area of a city, they join them and work together for the glory of God. When a couple is faithful during training and serves others on the team, they empower this couple to lead others. As their teams live and practice what they believe in Christ, they together reject old assumptions and they hunger for righteousness rather than significance.

This is not without cost, as Elizabeth McLean has shared with us. At times she despairs because of the criticism leveled at her and Robert and the negative gossip about their support. She also feels disempowered by some teams and struggles with anxiety and defensiveness for Robert when he comes under attack. It is clear that in their leadership roles, they often suffer as they follow Christ. But in the end, both say, "Not I, but Christ." And they understand that success and significance are not about them; they are about "team" and following Jesus.

Clinical psychologist Betsy Barber sums up how meek leadership and suffering lead to what we truly want "in Christ": "Our desires define us: When we are shaken, we find out what our hearts' true desires are. We will know what we truly want, and therefore, who we truly are. And as we are shaken further, we are emptied out so that we may be filled with eternal things. God's desire is to give us the eternal things—to have His Kingdom fill our hearts."[14]

## REFLECTION QUESTIONS

- What are two or three compelling hungers (called "cravings" [CEB] in James 1) that drive your work and ministry?
- How do you respond when things in your life seem out of control?
- Why are we tempted to struggle alone with these cravings rather than seek support in the body of Christ?
- What daily habits do you have in Christ to submit your desires and hungers to him?

14. Betsy Barber, "God Shakes Things Up," 2020 Advent Project (Biola University), December 5, 2020, http://ccca.biola.edu/advent/2020/#day-dec-5.

# 9

# Balancing Convictions, Rights, and Loving Others in Christ

SHERWOOD G. LINGENFELTER

Yet I hold this against you [the church in Ephesus]: You have forsaken the love you had at first. Consider how far you have fallen! Repent and do the things you did at first. If you do not repent, I will come to you and remove your lampstand from its place. (Rev. 2:4–5)

Do not be afraid of what you [the church in Smyrna] are about to suffer. I tell you, the devil will put some of you in prison to test you, and you will suffer persecution for ten days. Be faithful, even to the point of death, and I will give you life as your victor's crown. (Rev. 2:10)

The question of this chapter is: How can we balance our convictions, rights, and love in Christ in our relationships with the members of our multinational team? We begin by examining how Satan may nurture our "self-representation" of these convictions and rights to divide members of the body of Christ who have been called by God to serve together for God's mission. Sigve Tonstad, in his book *Revelation*, observes that the churches of Ephesus and Smyrna faced a

89

"discrepancy between self-representation and reality," and "most of the issues enumerated are internal, intra-Christian issues."[1] Examining all seven churches, he finds a pattern of false claims: those in Ephesus claimed to be apostles, those in Pergamum to be Jews, those in Thyatira to be prophets, and those in Laodicea to be rich (Rev. 2:2, 9, 20; 3:17). But none of them were actually those things![2]

Most importantly, the text identifies Satan as the major agent of deception in all seven of the churches, dividing the body of Christ by means of internal disagreements, mistrust, and sinful behaviors. It is not our purpose to exegete these texts here but rather to heed the warning—"you have forsaken the love you had at first"—and the prescription—"repent" and "be faithful"—given by Jesus to correct the situations. The question of this chapter comes from the text on Ephesus: How do we balance our convictions between who we think we are and the reality of our love for Jesus Christ?

### Blindness in Self-Perception

During my first mission assignment in Brazil in 1977, my SIL colleagues introduced me to some of the friendly faculty at the University of Brasília. As we conversed, I was stunned by their anxieties about Brazil's relationship with the United States. They spoke of how the United States had interfered in Brazil's political processes and of the large influence of US corporations on Brazil's economy. One man even said he was afraid of a military invasion by the US. In my "self-representation," I declared that such intervention was totally contrary to the US identity, which valued political and religious freedom. In response, they asked, "What about your invasion of Cuba at the Bay of Pigs in 1961 against Fidel Castro?" At that moment, I defended my self-representation, certain that my view of America and my personal position were truthful and accurate. I excused the invasion of Cuba as a legitimate response to a communist plot against "democracy."

---

1. Tonstad, *Revelation*, 100–101.
2. Tonstad, *Revelation*, 83.

Only in reflection, years later, did I grasp clearly the discrepancies between my self-perception, my self-representation, and the reality that these men and women had experienced in Brazil and in other Central and South American nations. Many Latin American leaders and common people judge such US foreign policy as "imperialism"— extending its dominant position and using political policies, economic pressure, and foreign aid to support US interests.

Why do I begin this chapter with such a story? According to Revelation 12:9 (CEB), the ancient serpent, Satan, is the "the deceiver of the whole world," and part of his deceptive work is inciting humans to dominate, subjugate, and conquer others—behaviors endemic in human history. Such domination inevitably forces others into subservient roles (as subjects or slaves) for personal and national gain. We see this evidenced as early as the biblical stories of Joseph and Moses in Egypt.

In the twentieth century, the legacy of nineteenth-century colonialism shaped two major world wars and the formation of nation-states around the world after World War II. Some of those nation-states are known as Anglophone and Francophone Africa. The Atanda case study in chapter 13 describes how the ministry of mobilization by Zion World Prayer and Missions—out of its Anglophone context— has faced difficulties from Francophone church leaders, political leaders, and jihadists, who at times incite resistance and assault against God's people and ministry.

### "We Are Right, We Are Good": Convictions about Identity

We must ask, then, how Satan seeks to undermine the mission of the global church through such political and economic polarities. The fact is that all mission recruits come from specific nation-state contexts, and we bring our cultural and family legacies and identities with us to this work. In chapter 10, Penny Bakewell describes how her British identity negatively impacted her relationship with North East Indian team members. In chapter 12, Matthew Crosland describes how Papua New Guineans viewed all expatriates as "older brothers" in their partnership. Whether we come from North America, South America, Europe, Africa, Australia, Oceania, or Asia, we accede to the polarities of our nations of origin, and at the same time we expect our team members to accept us and work with us for cross-cultural teamwork.

As I (Sherwood) have examined the cases presented in chapters 10 through 13, I have found a pattern in the internal, intra-Christian issues that Satan is using to divide the body of Christ. Our enemy uses our mutual histories—those of nation-states, denominations, and local communities—to divide us internally by mutual "self-perceptions" that lead us to believe we have the right either to dominate or to resist the domination of others—and he thereby destroys our "first love" for Christ and his global church.

## "The Right" to Dominate: Two Case Studies

The McLeans (see chap. 11) describe the blessing and privilege of equipping missionary recruits from the United States, Central and South America, and Europe to serve in Central Asia. The McLeans' mission organization was founded in the United States and is associated with independent church networks around the world. Because it is an American organization, competition is normal among its leaders, and command-and-control "domination" is often the default leadership practice, particularly in the churches—a practice that reflects the US national origin and history. The organization's sending board, which is thoroughly North American, has assigned members to lead and equip new recruits who choose to partner with them for the work of church planting across Central Asia. All of these missionary recruits come with identities deeply anchored in the cultures of the family, church, and nation-state that supported and sent them.

Martins Atanda (author of chap. 13)—the founder of Zion World Prayer and Missions in Nigeria—has worked for twenty-five years to mobilize leaders and churches in nations that were once French and British colonies across Central Africa. Nigeria is one of the "success stories" in Africa—dominant economically and politically—and "big man" leadership is the norm, blending African practices of "chief-led kingdoms" and the country's British colonial legacy. France and Britain continue to influence the surrounding nations, both economically and politically. As we have seen, the Francophone nations are particularly resistant to Nigerian leadership and influence.

## "The Right" to Resent and Resist

What the McLean and Atanda case studies have in common are team members committed to Christ and to his mission but wounded—emotionally, socially, and economically—by the domination they have experienced from the nations represented by the mission leaders. As a consequence, when some encounter anything in their training they deem "unreasonable" or "not the way we do things," they feel "subject" and thus experience emotional resentment and respond with resistance.

Latin Americans may resent "working for" Americans, and Francophone Africans may resist "teaching" by Nigerians; in either case, team members doubt the philosophy and framework used by their leaders to define teamwork. In some cases, these people tend to ignore the leaders and their training. Atanda reports how some church leaders have rejected his teaching and some team members have decided to go their own way or to return to their denominational ministries.

Attitudes—acquired in people's home communities—seep into the body of Christ, leading to conflict about teamwork. Some members, in day-to-day relationships, may assume (sometimes falsely) that Christians from "imperialist" nations have the same values and attitudes as the economic and political leaders of these nations. When it comes to crises, however small, the temptation to resist and do things "against" leaders or team members is great. Further, when confronted with questions about which members may disagree, some team members may judge and condemn their leaders, while others may support them. The McLeans report that some who resist just "give up," while others reject the team or leaders and "act against" them.

Atanda found that some church leaders attend his prayer tours and teaching but go away and do nothing. Others get excited, join the ministry outreach, and even commit to become missionaries "on partial support." However, when the spiritual opposition is great, some disappear to find their own ministries. In both of these case studies, ministry leaders and teams have been compelled to face the discrepancy between their self-representation as a "team" and the reality of the internal issues that have divided them.

## Repentance and Recovering Your First Love in Christ

In his message to the church at Ephesus, Jesus admonishes the Ephesians, "Consider how far you have fallen! Repent and do the things you did at first" (Rev. 2:5).

"Consider how far you have fallen!" If we look at the details in this text, Jesus has praised the Ephesians for their deeds, their labor, their endurance; for refusing to tolerate evil people; for not becoming weary. But these very good attributes have so consumed them that they have fallen—so much so that they must evaluate "how far." The items of praise in this text should be familiar to us. Most Western mission organizations place a high value on hard work and the deeds of ministry; they measure the time spent, the quality of work done, and team progress toward the vision, and their annual objectives involve assessing the growth in churches, in converts, or in other mission outcomes. How many organizations annually assess team effectiveness in the work of faith, the labor of love, and perseverance in hope—"the things you did at first"? In the pages that follow, we reflect on how the McLean and Atanda case studies have focused on these "first things," yet in culturally and spiritually unique and distinctive ways.

The Saturday before I drafted this chapter (in December 2020), I connected with Martins Atanda in Sokoto, Nigeria, via a video call. He made time for me at the end of the first of three weeks of fasting and prayer. Atanda's team spent the first three days of the week fasting with a break for food in the evening, then two days continuously without food, the sixth day breaking fast with worship, and the seventh day traveling to the next regional site. Atanda, his "core team" members, and supporting cast spent this time praying for workers, churches, and believers in their harvest fields who were suffering from persecution by jihadists. These jihadists had prevented Christian families—many without food—from harvesting their fields, driving them from their homes and villages to places of safety. This work of prayer—focusing on Christ—continued during the following weeks, with core team members leading a second and third week of prayer in their respective regions of ministry. They recognized that without prayer and the power of the Holy Spirit, they have no hope for unity, nor strength to endure the suffering to come.

For Atanda and his core team members, the labor of love is sacrificial giving and working alongside participants who come from towns characterized by poverty and lack; since very few have means of support, the mission and core teams charge nothing for training and provide food, clothing, and essential materials to supplement the farms and provide family support for participants. They also seek support from global partners for water-supply projects and other projects when needed. By their persistence in prayer and by training cycles each year, they emphasize an unflagging hope in Jesus Christ, encourage faith and endurance in times of suffering, and rejoice together when Satan's work is thwarted and when seeds sown bud and show promise of becoming fruitful.

During the same time period, Robert and Elizabeth McLean were visiting "satellite team" members in different locations in Central Asia, engaging with members about Scripture, and affirming them "as God's chosen people, holy and dearly loved" (Col. 3:12). Their commitment has been to embrace members individually and work with them to allow Scripture to define their lives together. Elizabeth confesses the problems revealed in their cultural and mission history and at the same time describes their repentance and actions to refocus "in Christ":

> Our global organization inadvertently fosters a competitiveness that is visible on the field. On the surface it does not seem harmful, but

over time it can turn into jealousy, comparison, bringing others down to size, and maintaining *my spot* in the pecking order. In order to combat this, we must become a filter through which new members experience an in-Christ team committed to in-Christ responses to the world's culture and to our own organizational culture. The only way to achieve such transformation is through "immersion in Scripture"—a "word filter" that screens out the fruit of the flesh. As leaders, we have failed them on more than one occasion—sometimes not giving people a fair assessment or a fair opportunity to grow—thus denying them the opportunity for growth by experiencing in-Christ community.[3]

Given the multinational character of the satellite teams working in Central Asia, the McLeans work diligently to put others first, and they invite team members to do the same. Even when their frustration over internal conflict is high, Elizabeth writes, "If my inner life is rightly oriented in Christ, then cross-cultural issues are less of a threat. My expertise as a leader is less important and, in fact, secondary to the way I live and lead in Christ." For Robert and Elizabeth, "Our hope is grounded in Jesus's faithfulness and his promise to be with us until his return."[4] In times of internal conflict and distress—an ever-present reality—their hope in Christ is the antidote to giving up and going their own way.

## Embrace, Trust, Empower

In his message to the church at Smyrna, Jesus admonishes these church members, "Be faithful, even to the point of death, and I will give you life as your victor's crown" (Rev. 2:10). Being faithful is best understood as action: concrete acts of hard work living in surrender and obedience to Christ. Again, comparing the ministries of the McLeans and of Atanda, each has developed distinctive patterns of embracing, trust-building, and empowering (see table 9.1). Atanda testifies that "we always did research before we entered a community—mapping,

3. Elizabeth McLean (pseudonym), interview by Sherwood G. Lingenfelter, December 2, 2020.
4. Elizabeth McLean, interview.

## Table 9.1
### In-Christ Actions: Embrace, Trust, Empower

| In-Christ Actions | McLean Case Study | Atanda Case Study |
| --- | --- | --- |
| Embracing | Share stories, burdens<br>Discuss issues | Discern needs, give sacrificially<br>Focus on Jesus as healer, savior |
| Trust-building | Affirm "together in Christ"<br>Confess "judgments"<br>Embrace the "forgiven" | Mobilize prayer tours<br>Equip local people for local outreach<br>Display gratitude, even when people fail |
| Empowering "partners" | Give away authority<br>Affirm unity in Christ | Undertake cycles of prayer<br>Release and encourage partners |

discerning obvious public and personal needs, and analyzing each community so we knew how to approach them with love and the gospel. We always tried to approach them where they are soft, serving a felt need to bless them."[5] But to be faithful is always to share the gospel, and to do that, Atanda's team used the God's Story Project version of the *Jesus Film*, which from beginning to end is about Jesus inviting people to follow him. To build trust and avoid a violent reaction to the film, they screened it in parts, over three days, approximately one hour each day. If, in their research, they discovered that people were afflicted with chronic sickness and fear, they projected the section that shows Jesus healing the sick and casting out demons. Atanda concludes, "Through our research, we usually avoid most of the violent reactions. But when such a reaction occurs, you just pack up your stuff and get out of town."

For Elizabeth McLean, being faithful was often a battle about internal issues on the teams. She testifies:

My biggest battle is fighting knee-jerk reactions and quick fixes to solve people's problems. I can see what issues they're facing and have seen solutions that work. This chronic mindset of fixing people turns into rumination for me . . . and before I know it I'm grasping to exert control in people's lives.

5. Quotations in this paragraph are from Martins Atanda, personal interviews by Sherwood G. Lingenfelter, November 2020.

It is not my job to fix; only the Holy Spirit can do that. I can steward, ask good questions, be a non-anxious presence. If I choose to partner with the Holy Spirit, it will be a longer road of allowing the Spirit to move deeply into people's inner will and into areas of their walk with God that are not whole. The process will also bring me to a place of dependence and trust in the Holy Spirit at work, even when I do not see it.[6]

Elizabeth and Robert McLean have adopted strategies of action very similar to what Bakewell describes in chapter 10: they engage personally with team members, inviting them to share their stories and listening carefully without judgment or surprise that might signal disapproval. This takes significant time, but investing in people, bearing their burdens with them, and discussing possible responses are their work of leadership.

The McLeans have given the highest priority to building trust and empowering others because we are all together "in Christ," a notion that radically levels the playing field. They conclude that teams in missions are not spaces for self-promotion or ladder climbing but arenas in which our togetherness is expressed in concrete acts. They also conclude that building trust must include actions of confession and forgiveness. Elizabeth describes this aspect of their personal journey in leadership:

Our experience with Latin [American] brothers—and at times with North Americans who come from various Pentecostal backgrounds—is discomfort and hesitant incredulity. They have not experienced leaders leading with vulnerability or transparency in public settings. They are surprised by our willingness to express uncertainty and to open the floor for participatory leadership that impacts the direction of a team. Very few will openly communicate a difficult moment or invite team members to offer public criticism or to publicly repent if they have misled. In their context, they expect leaders to always portray power—everything under control—and cannot imagine a humble confession: "I am struggling to hear from God."[7]

6. Elizabeth McLean, interview.
7. Elizabeth McLean, interview.

Together, Robert and Elizabeth seek to model how confession and forgiveness are biblically based actions that—when we obey Jesus—lead team members to grasp experientially that "we are together in Christ."

The McLeans have also made empowerment a core feature of their mentoring and equipping ministry. Elizabeth tells the story of how a satellite team resolved the "problem" of holding communion in a house church plant:

> The southern European leaders suggested that they include an occasional "communion" in their worship. The South Americans—from a Latin "high church" background—struggled with the idea of "house church" and objected to "communion" without an "ordained pastor" leading. The leaders listened—then, over several weeks, discussed together biblical reasons for or against. After reaching an agreement, the South American couple took first responsibility to host, and they led the worship and communion enthusiastically.[8]

As teams consistently live out what they say they value, they work to break down assumptions. Later, when the South Americans separated to become leaders of their own satellite team, they held communion in every evening worship. As Robert concludes in chapter 11, at the end of the day, all of us should discover, as we work with one another, "Behold—new creation!"

Martins Atanda is about teamwork with local people for local and regional outreach (see table 9.1). He and "core team" members work hard to build up local leadership and to empower these people to follow their example as they, the leaders, follow Christ. Centering their ministry on prayer—which cycles from the core team to regional and international teams—they renew their reliance on the power of Jesus to heal, to forgive, and to lead people into an abundant and eternal life. And in situations where opposition forces them to "get out of town," they express deep gratitude to those who have suffered in the name of Jesus—as in Smyrna, "the devil will put some of you in prison to test you, and you will suffer persecution for ten days" (Rev. 2:10).

8. Elizabeth McLean, interview.

### Servant Leadership—a Discrepancy?

As I conclude this chapter, I return to the opening question: What is the discrepancy between our self-representation (of church and mission) and the reality we face? In cross-cultural teamwork, most leaders subscribe to the ideal of servant leadership, but if you ask team members, many see a discrepancy between a leader's self-representation and the reality of how this leader leads on a day-to-day basis. That discrepancy may arise from a failure to grasp the substantive cultural disconnects in the ministry or from a failure to deal emotionally and spiritually with one's frustration and disappointment with team members. Atanda tells a story about how he stepped out with others, thinking to model the practice of ministry, and experienced cultural disconnect:

> Early in our ministry we led a church planting initiative in a town in Niger. In our research, we learned that they needed clean water, and so we provided a well through our partner. After the well was finished, we started conversations with individuals or small groups about how to prevent sickness through personal hygiene. I started a conversation with a friendly local woman, who I did not know, about the health benefits of taking a shower. When local men heard about my conversation with this woman, they angrily gathered to beat me.[9]

Forewarned by his team, who explained that men had several wives and women took showers only before meeting their husbands at night, Atanda immediately began to apologize, explaining that he was teaching about sickness and the hygienic benefit of taking a shower daily. Learning from this near-tragic mistake, he never tried to teach a woman alone again. Instead, he found a local nurse, had her dress in appropriate clothing as a health practitioner, and invited her to come and do the same teaching. Today there are five churches in that community: the water and health ministry of service opened doors, and the Spirit of God did the rest.

Robert and Elizabeth McLean believe deeply in servant leadership. When new members first hear Robert speak and lead as a servant, they voice negative responses out of their own "self-representation

9. Atanda, interview.

of leadership": "I have never heard a leader say something like that," "you are showing too much weakness," "we don't know what to do with this." After weathering their initial shock about his risk of both transparency and weakness, Robert turns to focus on gratitude to God and reliance on God's steadfastness: "We follow a strong God." Yet the challenge of daily life with these fully human teammates threatens the McLeans' "servant" commitment. Elizabeth confesses her emotional and spiritual disconnect: "We know that when people are really hurting, they often misunderstand or have distorted memories about what happened. In such situations, they accuse us of making life harder, when we think we are trying to help. I get deeply hurt, and react in anger, when 'my will' is threatened by 'their will.' Out of that frustration, anger, resentment, I find myself sinning against them—using my power, withdrawing my support, becoming inaccessible when they need me."[10]

The McLeans and Atanda, in very different ways, have embodied servant roles among the people they were training for ministry. Each took significant risks, each exposed personal weaknesses, and each learned how better to serve and how to be faithful "even to the point of death." Yet, on their own strength, they could not sustain that servant attitude and heart. Elizabeth concludes, "I confess that at these times I desperately need periods of solitude in Scripture, allowing the Holy Spirit to work in my life—and in those with whom I am distressed—so that transformation is possible for us all."[11] To restore their "first love," leaders and teams must "repent in Christ" and then commit anew to "be faithful" to the work of faith, the labor of love, and steadfast hope. Whether engaged or waiting, they must allow the Holy Spirit to do this work among them: "We who are powerful need to be patient with the weakness of those who don't have power, and not please ourselves. Each of us should please our neighbors for their good in order to build them up. Christ didn't please himself, but, as it is written, *The insults of those who insulted you fell on me*" (Rom. 15:1–3 CEB).

10. Elizabeth McLean, interview.
11. Elizabeth McLean, interview.

## REFLECTION QUESTIONS

- What forms do domination and resistance take in the nations represented on your team?
- How does the self-representation of team members fall short of the reality they are facing?
- How often do you consider as a team your "first love" for Jesus and how you are living and loving now?
- How important is servant leadership on your team, and what do you see as potential discrepancies between God's model and your team's practice?

PART 3

# Five Leaders, Four Journeys, Four Metaphors of Leadership for "Mission with" in Christ

The chapters that follow, written by our contributing authors, provide the detailed case studies that have been analyzed in the previous chapters. The cases all present their authors' views of their respective journeys meeting the challenge of wicked problems in their teamwork. Each chapter identifies specific biblical metaphors of leadership—shepherd, servant, steward—that guided the authors in their respective journeys as they sought to follow the leading of the Holy Spirit. The authors all worked with very different multinational teams, confronting challenges that lasted for months, years, and even decades. No leader was perfect; they all responded in ways unique to their nationality, personality, educational preparation, and ministry experience. Each has a distinctive personality, a unique experience with Jesus Christ, and a very specific calling in ministry. And each participates in "one body and one Spirit, just as you were called to one hope when you were called; one Lord, one faith, one baptism; one God and Father of all, who is over all and through all and in all" (Eph. 4:4–6).

The beauty of these chapters is that no two wicked problems are the same, and there is no catalog of steps or tasks to address them. The leaders do not rely on a "learning culture" textbook or a "learning leadership" textbook. They all have varied ministry training, and all have studied the challenges of learning and living with people outside their own culture and mother tongue, but the journeys of engaging their wicked problems are unique to each.

What we hope you gain from reading these chapters is encouragement—through the Scriptures and the leading of the Holy Spirit, all have the essential resources to walk worthy of their calling in Christ Jesus. We hope that you learn to question your assumptions and to listen to and learn from the body of Christ given to you for ministry. We hope that you discover how biblical metaphors may guide you in difficulty and uncertain times. We pray that you may discover new ways to lead within Christ's body, becoming an effective ligament enabling members of the household in which you serve to do their work. We hope that you recognize common trials, errors, and adjustments; small steps forward; the joy of answered prayer; and the fruit of the Spirit in these stories.

These chapters also reveal ways of approaching wicked problems that you may not have yet experienced and that you may wish to explore further. We provide footnotes in the text to guide you to additional sources that may be helpful.

# 10

# Enabling In-Christ Participation

PENNY BAKEWELL

Think for a moment about the last leadership team meeting you led or attended. Who were the *two* people who participated the most in that meeting? I wonder how many of you reading this already have the names of those two people in your mind.

One research study that analyzed videos of a series of meetings showed that in the majority of those meetings, 60 percent of the participation came from just two people.[1] That means that those meetings were dominated by the opinions, knowledge, and worldviews of two people. Is this characteristic of your meetings? Can you name the two who talk the most?

In the last decade, SIM has placed increasing emphasis on the formation of multicultural, multiskilled teams to accomplish its mission and purpose. However, if we are to benefit from the diversity, knowledge, and creativity of multicultural and multiskilled teams, we also need to have multi-engagement and multi-participation in

1. Gorse et al., "Meetings," 919–20.

the sharing of ideas in our discussions and in the decision-making process.

Why? Why do we believe that participation is so important?

## The Wicked Problem—Silence or Participation?

We believe that everyone in Christ is equally valued and valuable. God can choose to speak at different times through every one of us as we seek to discern his will together. We believe that creative thinking comes from the wealth of ideas that result from the diversity of our cultures, our personalities, our experiences, our knowledge, and our histories. It is a concern when people with experience in the area under discussion stay silent. As a Korean colleague once told me, "There is wisdom in our silence!" How do we tap into that? Everyone has ideas, but so often they stay locked up in our team members' minds.

In any team, but particularly in a multicultural team, it is only as everyone engages that we can know that what we are discussing is relevant and important to everyone. We can't know what a silent room is telling us, because silence tells us different things depending on how we interpret that silence.

When I first took on the role of director of the SIM team in Ghana, to say I felt completely out of my depth is an understatement. I said to a colleague, "My Bible verse is going to be Proverbs 17:28—'Even a fool when he keeps silent is considered wise!'" But silence does not help us in leadership meetings. We cannot know unless we hear.

Participation is important. Participation of the many leads to a greater sense of joint responsibility. It is much more likely that engaged and animated team leaders will engage and animate their teams around a decision that has been made, motivating sustained and sustainable strategies of ministry. If we are to benefit from our multicultural and multiskilled teams, we need to encourage multi-engagement and multi-participation.

SIM Ghana is a diverse team—eight different nationalities are represented in a team of twenty-six missionaries. One in every three missionaries is from a different country and culture. However, up until 2018 we were (unintentionally) a multinational team working monoculturally. The SIM Ghana missionaries from North East India served together in a rural town northeast of Tamale. In the Sisaala region, the missionaries were all from the West—the UK, Canada, and the US. Only in Tamale itself was the team truly multicultural. In 2018 this all changed when the SIM Ghana team was blessed with four new missionary families, two from Ethiopia and one each from the Central African Republic and South India. Thanks to these new members and the movement of other team members, this diverse team became a multicultural team working multinationally.

As well as being a diverse team, we were now also a new team, new to each other and new to Ghana. Only four of us had been in Ghana for more than ten years, and eleven of our missionaries had been in Ghana for less than three years. We were early on in our diversity journey. Our leadership team of eight is, as of 2021, made up of four nationalities—British, South Korean, North East Indian, and Canadian. The many nationalities represented on our team mean the leadership team is going to become even more diverse in the future.

### The Silence Challenge

In our leadership team meetings, I experienced the "silence" challenge among the eight team members. People who were normally outgoing, confident, and engaged outside the conference room became introverted, silent types as soon as they entered the room.

I set out to find out why. I wanted to discover what helped people within the leadership team participate in meetings and what hindered them from doing so. What was the reason for the quite dramatic change in them? I believed that once I knew the answers, I could change both the way I prepared for meetings and the way I led the meetings to enhance participation. I would have a nice list of useful points that I could put into action—and, in a sense, I did discover action items. But I also found out something much more valuable.

Jesus challenges us, "I am the good shepherd; I know my sheep and my sheep know me" (John 10:14). So do I *know* my sheep? If we want multiethnic, multiskilled leaders to engage, we must get to know our leaders and let them get to know us. We must not assume we know; we must know we know. This is the guiding principle that I used to address the silence challenge: *Get to know your leaders. Don't assume you know; know you know.*

Familiarity with a person is not the same as knowing a person. The more diverse we become, the less likely it is that our assumptions about people will be correct. The more diverse we become, the less likely it is that our interpretations of each other's actions will match the actual reasons behind those actions. We can truly know only if we ask—and so I did.

## What Helps and Hinders Participation?

"I am not what you see. I am what time and effort and interaction slowly unveil."[2]

Two key questions shaped my inquiry: What helps you participate in idea sharing? and What hinders your participation?

The entire team said that understanding the background of an issue and having time to think through the issue before meeting were key to helping them express ideas. Brainstorming during the meeting and batting around ideas that had not been thought through beforehand was not comfortable for everyone. It was especially uncomfortable for our colleagues from India and Korea. For them, thinking out loud in the context and the formality of leadership meetings was particularly difficult. The expectation in their cultures is that a great deal of thought and preparation will go into any contribution before they are expected to share. They will have discussed it with their local teams first—with the people the idea or issues affect. Once they have listened locally, the ideas that they bring to the conference table will be the ideas of their group, their team—not their own individual ideas.

As I listened, I found that culture was not the only factor that influenced the level of participation. One of the leaders from the West

2. Goodrich, *Slaying Dragons*, 125.

said, "I need time and space to think. Once people start bringing forward ideas, I struggle to engage, because my mind is still thinking about the issue or the question. Having time to think about the issues before we meet would really help me."

Not everyone will come prepared: one of the team members needed the stimulation of interaction with others. "I need the excitement of others around the issue to inspire me." This works well for her and leads to some incredibly creative thinking because, as she admits, she is fearless—she speaks her mind and is quite happy to bring out ideas without having given much thought to them. At times her thinking has been way outside the box but beneficial, increasing the level of creative thinking in the room.

We need the creative, "way outside the box" thinkers—just one or two! And we need to enable people to come prepared, to connect with their teams about the issues that concern them, if we are to help people to engage and participate and share ideas freely.

For others, it is essential to ask them for ideas—people from Korea and India will wait to be asked for their contribution. We must make sure we give them that opportunity. We mustn't assume that because they are silent, they don't have anything to say.

*Get to know your leaders. Don't assume you know; know you know.*

## The Challenge of Second Language

Given the diversity of cultures and therefore of languages within our team, I wanted to explore how to encourage the participation of those who were using their second language. Premeeting preparation was particularly important to them, and having clear explanations of the issues to be discussed was vital to that preparation.

The way the meeting is led is key to facilitating the participation of this important group. In order to enable people to keep up with the flow of the discussion, I found it essential to slow interactions down, to allow space for clarifying questions, and to summarize the main points of the discussion that were made. One person (whose first language was English) suggested that I write the issue on the whiteboard and then write down ideas as they came. This allows people to read what is being said—rather like providing subtitles. When the speed of interaction increases, second-language participants struggle. They need time first to hear what is being said and then to catch up and to think about what was said. Only then will they be ready and able to contribute. Writing things on the board provides thinking time by slowing down the pace of the interaction.

Interestingly, interruption was seen as rude by most people from most cultures—but not all and not always. For example, during brainstorming sessions, creative thinkers need to get their ideas out there, and so being able to interrupt in order to get another idea on the table was important to them lest they forget. However, interruption can be used as a model to prevent people from making their point. I would therefore recommend that in multilingual meetings, we avoid interruption. It is much harder to keep up with the flow of what is being said when others are cutting in.

*To summarize: we need to slow down the speed of interaction, provide time for clarifying questions and summary, and discourage interruption.*

One of our members, whose mother tongue is English, said, "Penny, you need to meet with those being invited for the first time well before the meeting. You need to tell them that their contribution is important." Several non-first-language speakers agreed. "Telling them that you are looking forward to hearing their contribution. Giving them the expectation that they will be asked for their ideas helps them to prepare with that expectation in mind." Premeeting preparation is important.

*Once the ideas are on the table, the important and creative part of selecting the best ideas—the ideas that help to address the issue—begins.*

## Can You Disagree—Directly, Indirectly, or Not at All?

What makes for fruitful, creative discussion? Agreement and disagreement, challenge and affirmation. Discussion of the pros and cons of an idea is where much of the creative thinking happens. James Plued-demann quotes Peter Drucker in his book *Leading across Cultures*: "The first rule of decision making is that one does not make a decision unless there is disagreement."[3] Challenge and disagreement are vital to better-worked outcomes; colleagues push each other to continually ask one another, "Is this the best way; is there a better way; is this the way that God is leading us?" Disagreement helps the team to think in different ways, to consider new ideas. If we want to benefit from our diversity, we need to disagree—if we don't disagree, then either we are all thinking the same way (unlikely) or we are keeping silent.

In Indian culture, you can challenge and disagree, but the way you do this is important. One team member said, "If I don't agree with someone's idea, I always begin by affirming the idea. I will say, 'That is a good idea, but I wonder if another idea might be. . . .' To disagree with someone directly is not good—it is seen as a personal attack, not just a difference of opinion." This indirect approach is common across relationship-oriented cultures. Currently among the nationalities in the SIM Ghana leadership team, most members prefer a quite indirect way of challenging.

In her book *The Culture Map*, Erin Meyer notes that while US and Canadian cultures are very direct in their communication, they are more indirect compared to other Western nations when it comes to giving negative feedback.[4] In a sense, disagreement is negative feedback—you don't think the idea is the best idea. However, Americans and Canadians will still come across as very direct in their disagreement when they are compared to colleagues from Korea and India, for whom preserving harmony and saving face is central.[5]

Personality and generation play a role in whether someone feels comfortable with disagreeing. A Canadian colleague admitted that, for her, the difficulty with disagreeing with someone's contribution related to her personality and her generation. She said, "I ask myself the question, 'Do I feel I am the one who needs to disagree?' If it is

3. Plueddemann, *Leading across Cultures*, 195.
4. Meyer, *Culture Map*, 70.
5. Meyer, *Culture Map*, 200.

important, then someone else will do it. I don't like confrontation, and for me to disagree with someone means that I am devaluing the person, not just the idea." She said, "In my generation, everything is personal; everything says something about who you are and is part of your identity. So disagreement is felt very personally."

Once again, the big takeaway from these conversations was that we must take time to get to know our leaders—*don't assume you know; know you know*. Since asking "Can we disagree with one another?," I have wondered whether it would have been better to ask, "How do you express an opinion that is different from others'?" Perhaps the word *disagreement* is too loaded. Regardless, I was beginning to realize that we needed to revisit the value of challenge and disagreement as a leadership team if we were going to have creative discussions that celebrate diversity of views and ideas. We needed to decide together how we would challenge ideas to enable people to fully participate.

## Surprise—Hierarchy and Inhibitions to Disagreement

Given the number of missionaries coming from high-context cultures, I wanted to find out how hierarchy affects communication and, in particular, disagreement. Can you disagree with *anyone*? Does position or hierarchy change your ability to disagree? My Korean colleague responded, "Penny, as the director, if you make a suggestion, it's not a suggestion! It is going to happen, and no one is going to challenge you. Your role, therefore, is to add your affirmation to decisions that have been decided by the group. If you challenge someone's idea, that will be the end of that idea." Clearly this was worth knowing as a leader!

For those from the UK and Canada, hierarchy doesn't stop us from disagreeing, but it does affect how we disagree and how free we are with our disagreement. We tend to filter our words and play down what we are saying in order to avoid looking like we know more than those above us—we feel less free. So hierarchy does still have influence in less hierarchical cultures. However, to the Korean, you have insulted the boss just by disagreeing.

When I put this question of hierarchy to a colleague from North East India, his answer floored me. His wife, who had been listening, came across to him and whispered into his ear. She then left the room. He looked down thoughtfully and sighed.

Ah, Penny, you need to understand—people from the UK and from the US have a mentality of victor, of conqueror. We from India have a mentality of victim. We are now free, but in our hearts, we are not free. When the British colonized our land, it left a deep effect. It is hard for us to think that we are equal and our opinions are as valid as those from the West. We find it hard to disagree with someone if they are from the UK or US, and we may not bring a good idea out because we think that the idea is not good—we think that those from the UK and the US, their ideas are always better. We used to be ruled and protected by our chiefs, but then the British soldiers came and they told our chiefs what to do. So now we have this mentality that says, "Tell me what to do."

These two people are emerging leaders—courageous, passionate about their service, and with enormous potential. Yet it is true: within the conference room, he is quiet. Before I asked him about the effect of hierarchy, I never would have guessed that the reason this young man felt unable to contribute was because of our history—I am British and he is from North East India. *Get to know your leaders. Don't assume you know; know you know.*

Imagine how impossible it is for him to go against the tide in a discussion. We were talking about where to have our meetings and the possibility of moving them north, where everyone but I lived. Everyone agreed that we should look into it—everyone apart from those who were silent! That evening I was talking to this same couple. The wife looked at her husband, and he nodded. "Penny," she said, "I love coming to Accra—it's the only time we get a break from ministry." I gently said to her husband, "Wow, we needed to hear this voice." But he explained that he could never use the need for a vacation as a good reason to change the minds of the majority. Vacation wasn't cultural, and disagreeing with the majority—regardless of the reason—was next to impossible for him. Yet it was a voice, an opinion, that we needed to hear.

Did you notice that this man's wife spoke through him? That was interesting. I asked, "What would happen if both you and your wife were in leadership meetings? How would she contribute?" "It's true, she would ask my permission to speak, or she would allow me to speak on her behalf," he replied. So I asked, "What would happen if you didn't agree with what she wanted to say?" "I would tell her I don't agree and she would not speak." We would not hear her contribution. One of our team leaders had shared with me about this: "I am trying to get our young wife from India to be part of our discussions." This young wife is educated, extroverted, a people person. Learning that wives from both North East and South India will speak through their husbands helped us better understand and honor their preferred way of being heard. The wife will talk through her husband.

*Get to know your leaders. Don't assume you know; know you know.*

### So What? What Is the Application of This Knowledge?

Premeeting preparation enables people to think through and prepare what they want to contribute; it enables them to engage the local team that the issue affects. This is important to people from collective cultures, and actually it is important for those of us from individualist cultures to work more strongly with a sense of team. This means that preparation material needs to be provided in good time to allow the leaders to engage with their teams.

At the beginning of the meeting, it's important to set ground rules. I presented the findings above (from the results of the interviews) to our leadership team at a training seminar. Together, we made a list of guiding principles that we would commit to in order to enable everyone to participate in meetings. At the beginning of each leadership meeting, these guidelines are read aloud as we commit to hold each other accountable to them during the meeting:

- We are all equal in Christ.
- Everyone's opinion is valuable.
- God speaks through us all.

- Our diversity in culture, personality, history, and age gives great richness and creativity when we work together and participate fully.

Here are our commitments to one another:

1. We will share ideas freely, encourage open discussion, and frequently seek clarification of what we have heard to ensure that everyone has understood well.
2. We will speak slowly to enable full participation, using the whiteboard to record the main points.
3. We will summarize the main points frequently to help those for whom English is not their first language.
4. We will be aware of our body language and remember that body language is interpreted differently in different cultures.
5. We will affirm every contribution before suggesting an alternative view.
6. We will give opportunity for people to explain the reasons behind the questions being asked.
7. We will not be afraid of silence but instead welcome this space to think about what is being said.
8. We will ask for contributions, recognizing that waiting to be asked is expected in some cultures, and we will affirm the response "we have nothing to add" as a valid and valued response.
9. We will make room for more informal discussions and explore how best to do this.
10. We will avoid interrupting someone who is speaking but rather listen well.
11. We will build a community of trust, love, and friendship.
12. We will rejoice and be thankful for the blessing of pursuing God's will together.

As a team, we looked at how we would challenge well and discussed the value of disagreement as a method of pushing good ideas to be better ideas. Having this discussion further facilitated participation, because everyone understood the importance of challenge and committed to handling challenge in a way that affirmed the person and enhanced the discussion.

## In-Christ Knowing for "Mission with" Multiethnic Leaders

In all of this, I found that perhaps the most powerful method for enabling people to participate was *not* in the answers I discovered. Rather, the most powerful method for enabling participation was in the process of listening and learning in order to find those answers. When I heard Jesus's challenge—"I am the good shepherd; I know my sheep and my sheep know me" (John 10:14)—and began to put it into practice, the way I led the team began to change.

If we want multiethnic, multiskilled leaders to engage, we must get to know our leaders fully as people of a culture, community, and history different from our own. Don't assume you know; know you know—and allow them to get to know you as well. It was in those times together that my leaders experienced my listening to them, knowing them, and affirming them.

Let me close with one illustrative story. I have said that our young emerging leader from India was quiet during leadership meetings. Let me say, he *was* quiet. At the end of our visit, he said, "Penny, we really appreciate what you are doing. You really want to understand us." I didn't understand the impact that that time together would have until the next meeting. We were meeting together with our Ghanaian partner church to discuss some very challenging relationship issues that we were both experiencing. This young man was completely different; he was fully engaged throughout; he tackled the elephants in the room with candor and humor; he was incredibly courageous in what he said, saying things I could never have said—and because it came from him, our Ghanaian brothers listened. Unknowingly, I had stumbled upon the answer (or at least the beginning of the answer) to how this man and this couple could overcome the shackles of history to fully engage as an equally valued brother and sister in

Christ. Something had been unlocked in that time of seeking to know, to truly know. "I am not what you see. I am what time and effort and interaction slowly unveil."[6]

I believed, and still believe, that our team has a high level of trust. But even this did not overcome history, hierarchy, personality, or past hurt. We cannot know what holds people back and what helps people flourish in meetings, in ministry, and in life unless we take time and effort to interact—unless we ask. As we become more diverse, we cannot, indeed must not, rely on our assumptions to inform us.

We believe that everyone in Christ is equally valued and valuable, every voice worth hearing. We demonstrate that belief by taking the time to ask, to understand, to know our team leaders. To be shepherd leaders, we need to know our sheep and allow our sheep to know us.

## REFLECTION QUESTIONS

- Does a power distance gap (e.g., Britain and India) inhibit communication in your team?
- Does a gender difference (e.g., an Indian husband and wife) factor into communication?
- Does hierarchy (as in Korean culture) set boundaries for communication in your team?
- What have you learned from this case study about gaining in-Christ trust?

6. Goodrich, *Slaying Dragons*, 125.

# 11

# Equipping Multinational Ministry Teams

ROBERT AND ELIZABETH McLEAN*

We work together in recruiting, developing, and deploying missionaries from around the world to serve in ministry teams in Central Asia. As Americans, we came to the task with a particular set of assumptions related to the rugged individual, though already as young people that desire for independent achievement was tempered somewhat by our interest in leading a team and working with others. Over the years, God has grown in us a desire to see more non-US families and singles engaged with us in reaching the nations of Central Asia. Our current role provides just the opportunity to work toward that goal.

A number of years ago, it was determined that some intentional training at the front end of a cross-cultural ministry job could assist

---

* The authors are using pseudonyms to protect the identities of persons mentioned in the chapter.

in retention, longevity, and productivity in the field, so we set up "onboarding via training." The objective of the training programs, which range in length from a few months to a few years, is to equip men and women for long-term ministry in Central Asia. We focus on language learning and cultural understanding while developing practical knowledge and skills in communicating the gospel, discipling new believers, and assisting local churches in their efforts to reach out to their communities. We recruit people from diverse backgrounds— ranging from veterans of global work to people responding to their first call into mission. We have seen new colleagues arrive on the field as young as nineteen and as old as men and women looking to serve in retirement.

All of this happens in nations where the majority of the population is Muslim, and usually entire ethnic groups identify as Islamic. The goal is to see teams working among these people groups, so training is always carried out in a "team context" as well.

While the majority of our recruits have come from North America, we have participants from Latin America, Europe, and other parts of Asia as well. The total number of participants at any given time in a training environment may range from ten to a few dozen, so the structure of the team can vary quite a bit. When the training team is small, it models a small church planting team well; when it grows, it begins to feel quite different from a typical ministry-oriented small team in the field. In order to address this complexity, we often divide the team into smaller satellite teams, mimicking the size and feel of a long-term ministry team. These teams play together, pray together, engage in ministry together, and worship together.

Satellite teams are useful for training in a number of ways: They develop a shared vision and purpose for a given area of ministry and are able to pursue that ministry together. They also provide an environment of shared learning as everyone in the satellite is working to build foundational practices and knowledge. As in any team, satellite team members deal with conflict resolution, working together, following well, taking the lead in something, loving peer-to-peer and top-down accountability, and serving others in love.

## What Does It Mean to Be a Team?—a Wicked Problem

A family from a South American nation joined our team recently, and their presence on our team has helped shape our thinking about team life, working in multinational teams, and the model of conflict resolution in Christ. They came to us as veterans, having transferred from another nation. Our process for new workers to the region, irrespective of background, is to place them into the basic foundational work, so this family joined a satellite team and began language and cultural acquisition. The satellite team was made up of a few singles and one other family—all North Americans.

In multinational teams, it is sometimes difficult to discern the root of challenges that arise. Some challenges seem obviously rooted in cultural differences, particularly when teams are dealing with "hot" (relationship oriented) vs. "cold" (efficiency oriented) cultures or with high or low power distance (hierarchy vs. equality) cultures. At other times, the challenges we face with a colleague may be more personality-related, such as friction with someone more reserved or more outgoing than we are—such conflicts can happen irrespective of assumptions about one another's cultural norms. Often, our backgrounds, families of origin, and differing ministry experiences are helpful clues to discerning the source of a particular conflict.

In this particular situation, a few areas of challenge quickly revealed themselves with the addition of this South American family to our predominantly North American team:

- Personal life: The South American family had strong opinions about how to raise their child and how to order their lives, so rather than discussing or negotiating roles and team dynamics, they often approached their teammates with the language of "we have decided we will do this."
- Challenges in language: Operating in a multilingual environment provided a particular challenge. The training is conducted in English, and the South Americans had limited knowledge of English and frequently challenged the team to operate in a third language that nobody spoke or understood fluently.

- The purpose of the training: Because they had been field veterans, albeit in a different part of the world, the South Americans seemed to seek out the satellite team primarily for fellowship rather than for learning or training.
- Individual decision-making: The South American family made decisions regarding ministry on the basis of family interests without considering the leadership of the team or the cost to the team environment.

For example, the South Americans met their home country's ambassador and other officials. These connections led to potential business connections and a job opportunity. While this was not objectionable in and of itself, our approach had been to discuss life-altering decisions like this as a group, because when a member of a mission team takes a job, it changes the life not only of the individual with the job but also of the team, whose goals, vision, direction, and shared work are usually significantly impacted. The family discussed this potential job with the team but clearly implied that the decision was wholly theirs and would not have an impact on our team.

### Differing Perspectives about Being Part of a "Team"

In retrospect, it seems that our new colleagues were operating with a very different sense of what the word *team* means and how teams work, and we were operating with a mistaken assumption about their English fluency. In many situations they did what they preferred, arranging their lives according to their own felt needs. They did not include the team in processing decisions they regarded as personal. Simultaneously, because of their limited English skills, they tended to express themselves in stronger terms than they really felt. We heard "This is a line—do not cross it" when they might have intended "This is what we are thinking; what do you think?"

Much of what they experienced looks similar to how others process being in a new field or being completely new to the field. Feeling disjointed is common in the middle or late part of the first year, irrespective of national background. This experience reflects psychological and emotional responses to the myriad challenges of language acquisition, cultural adaptation, cross-cultural ministry adjustment, working on a team, and so on.

Unfortunately, owing to the clear differences in culture, it was easy for our colleagues to dismiss differences between them and us and their own stresses and challenges as the consequence of being with Americans rather than of being in a new cross-cultural environment. While all language acquisition happens in a non-English environment (100 percent in the local language), all other instruction in our training program, such as biblical or missiological study, happens in English. This creates an additional burden for non-native speakers, though it brings the benefit of allowing Asians, Europeans, Latin Americans, and others to study together.

For some of the cross-cultural and operating-as-a-team-related challenges, Erin Meyer's book *The Culture Map* proved very helpful. Her work repackages Geert Hofstede's studies for international businesses and teams, covering in an accessible way many of the points of friction we frequently see. Nevertheless, misunderstandings persist.

### In-Christ Strategies for Teamwork

The apostle Paul's desire to "regard no one from a worldly point of view" (2 Cor. 5:16) drives our approach to training new colleagues and working out the relationships present in multinational teams. The call in Philippians 2:5 to "have the same mindset as Christ Jesus" highlights both the type of mindset Paul hints at in 2 Corinthians and the source of that mindset. Rephrased, Philippians 2 says that we, the gathered community of God's people, should have a mindset among us that *belongs to us* (collectively) *in Christ*. Our nature "in Christ" is central to this idea, for the approach Paul advocates belongs to us *because* we are in Christ, and it also finds its source and is empowered *as* we are in Christ.

What does this look like in a multinational team? How can we resolve problems that arise from working with brothers and sisters from various nations and languages who bring their own assumptions with them?

Working through the complexities of cross-cultural life requires intentionality and discipline. This applies both to living as an expat in your host nation and to living in community on a multinational team. In fact, often team members discover that the multinational team is a greater source of missed expectations and cross-cultural stress than the host nation. This comes as a surprise to many because we do not expect that living alongside and working with other Christians will be difficult.

We begin by getting to know one another. This is an intentional practice that is included in training for new teams because it is so central to working together but is not always an obvious first step. There is power in simple activities: visiting someone at home to play a game in the evening or walking a teammate home, creating space for questions and observations to happen. We seek to create friendships—standing in the kitchen and working on canning hundreds of liters of spaghetti sauce or simply doing dishes together. We often sit on the floor playing with LEGO bricks with our teammates' kids—dads join in before you know it! The conversations that happen on the floor surrounded by children's toys have power of reassurance and of confirmation that you are living what you say from the pulpit.

We share our stories as part of team formation and then work to bear one another's burdens by sharing the ups and downs of our common life together. Our training sessions provide opportunities for group discussion and sometimes even debate, where team members engage with the wonderful mix of one another's theological differences, cultural expectations, and life experiences. In a multinational team environment, these moments of sharing and discussion become even more important, because mutual understanding helps create space for love and grace to be expressed to one another. The rubric of faith, hope, and love is a helpful lens through which to look at our work together.

## The Work of Faith: Calling, Prayer, Fasting

The work of faith in multinational team life is based on our assumption—our "leap of faith"—that God is involved not only in our lives but also in the lives of our colleagues. When difficulties arise, it is helpful to remember that my colleague is a child of God and a servant of the same Lord as I am. As such, this servant of the Lord standing in front of me, even when frustrating or puzzling to me in the moment, is someone precious to and beloved of God.

We have found that our Latin American colleagues have a very clear sense of calling. Often they have done their research before arriving, knowing among whom they want to live and where they want to spend their time reaching out. With Latin Americans from four different nations now joining us, we have seen their zeal and razor-sharp focus on evangelism over and over.

They are also, by and large, not afraid of prayer and fasting. When we have a regular rhythm of prayer and fasting as a community, they find that they are spiritually at home among us. We lean on them as leaders as we introduce North Americans to these practices, knowing that they can competently lead in these areas and normalize these spiritual practices that are often lacking in North American churches.

Expressing faith in the Lord in our daily lives requires something of us, of how we act and interact with others. Jesus calls us to obey everything he has commanded, and much of the instruction of the New Testament is oriented around how we live with one another. The work of faith bleeds into the labor of love, because expressing faith to our King in community necessarily involves expressing his love to one another, as John reminds us in his letter (1 John 4:7–8).

### The Labor of Love: Willing and Doing the Best for Others

As Paul envisions it, love turns out to be a concrete activity rather than an ephemeral feeling. Earlier we argued that love is intentional action. It is good works prompted by faith (Eph. 2:10). In our teams, we talk about love in terms borrowed and paraphrased from Dallas Willard, who would say that love is willing and doing what is best for someone else regardless of the cost to myself. In YouTube clips of his teaching, Willard talks about how loving God involves acting in God's best interest, and loving your spouse involves the same. Love is best exemplified in the life of Jesus, who models continually how to love God and love others in this way. Jesus did what was best for the Father, thus bringing honor to the Father through his life, teachings, and way of dying. In our ministry, we challenge one another to die to self in order to love others.

We saw this love in a Latin American couple. Within weeks of settling in, they began to venture into an urban territory known for extremism and for housing political immigrants who are part of terrorist cells known around the world, as well as persecuted ethnic groups. They had identified one of these people groups in their prayer before coming, and even as we presented the purpose of team training, their focus to bring the gospel to these people compelled them to take the first step—getting to know and to love these people.

The Lord also challenged us about our relative financial wealth in contrast with the relative poverty of our Latin American colleagues. In our early years of ministry, before we began training new missionaries, our very first Latin American team members had the business platform essential for long-term visas in the country but inadequate finances to live where we lived. We knew that God was calling us to work together and that God had provided a business for our brother, so we placed ourselves under his leadership and moved to the small town where our teammates had chosen to open this business. Given their marginal finances, we agreed to set up the office in our home and serve as the "guards." Our "office" became a very simple, very local setup that was comfortable, low-stress, and equally enjoyed by locals and our team. We stepped outside our American norm and discovered how very, very freeing it was to set up a ministry platform with a low start-up and maintenance budget.

Leaders make a big difference in multinational teams, because leaders set the tone for what love looks like. Are we serving our team from a posture of love? Do we truly put what is best for others first in our priorities and decision-making? It takes work to lead in this way, so Paul's description of it as "labor" is accurate. In a team, this pays rich dividends. When we believe someone else is acting in our best interests, we find within ourselves dramatic amounts of grace for them, even when something is muddled. When our teams are consistently maintaining a resolute intention to love and acting accordingly, they find that love truly does cover a multitude of sins (1 Pet. 4:8), as well as many lesser offenses.

## Steadfastness of Hope in Christ

Finally, while hope is essential in any mission endeavor, in multinational teams like ours it provides an antidote to giving up and going our own way in our own monocultural strength. Our hope is grounded in Jesus's faithfulness and his promise to be with us until his return. A sense of calling and purpose from the Lord in our work is something in which we can hope, and this hope calls us to be steady, to persist, and to work through challenges.

We have learned that when we live and act with hope "in Christ," he extends our influence beyond our dreams. For example, a couple from Central America visited our first ministry site in Central Asia. They were on a vision trip to explore possibilities for future ministry. We were traveling at that time, but we left keys with our colleagues so that the couple could use our apartment while they were in town. God confirmed his calling in their hearts, and six months later they arrived and began a wonderful season of ministry. The husband later told others that he had never been in a missionary home in Central America, and he was utterly amazed that we opened our home to them in our absence. Our Spirit-led act of in-Christ inclusion was an experience that motivated them over the years that followed and shaped our awareness of how others perceive us as Americans.

Our hope is in the death and resurrection of the exalted Christ, and yet we all have areas of weakness and doubt. When we see examples of faith, love, and hope in our colleagues, we are encouraged to persevere in moments that threaten our hope. The fervor and quick connections of the Latin American family that moved into extremist territory illustrate this point: their stories and the places where they were making inroads bolstered the spirits of the satellite team they were on and caused the whole team to gather around them and join them in evangelism in this neighborhood. Our mutual relationships with these Latin

American couples, who have such passion for evangelism to unreached people groups, enable all of us to flourish with steadfast hope.

### Trust and Empowerment: New Creation "in Christ"

Working toward success in multinational teams thus requires these fundamental values to be practiced in our lives. We work to express trust and to empower others, because we are all together "in Christ," a notion that radically levels the playing field. Teams in missions are not a space for self-promotion or ladder climbing but an arena in which our togetherness is expressed in concrete acts.

Many times, we come together with assumptions about one another. Overcoming the negative stereotypes usually requires more than willpower; it requires a willingness to be shaped into something beyond what our cultures value and to trust and serve one another in new ways. Multinational teams are an exceptional arena in which to overcome our assumptions about one another and to form long-lasting, trusting partnerships with people who are radically different from us. These teams are also complex and prone to failure because the journey toward unity in Christ is fraught with pitfalls.

We have had Latin Americans on our team who never wanted to learn English and resented working with us. Their pride in their own culture combined with an unwillingness to work "for" Americans made it difficult for them to see how a multinational team could work. While we worked to love and serve them, attempting to modify our communication to help them and contributing to funding for them, they never decided they were willing to shift their assumptions about us or their desire to be a part of what we were doing. Others have arrived with similar assumptions about American desires to dominate other nationalities but have discovered, over time, that the values of the kingdom of God *can* have an impact on team life, organizational structures, and leadership styles. As teams consistently live out what they say they value, they work to break down assumptions. At the end of the day, all of us should discover as we *work with one another*, "Behold—new creation!" (paraphrase of 2 Cor. 5:17).

## Leadership—Other-Oriented, Serve First

One aspect of how true partnership in missions is visible is through our leadership structures. Is leadership open to anyone, regardless of cultural background? Our teams have worked hard to give responsibility and authority away to partners from other nations. North Americans tend to expect to be leaders and often feel they are failing if they are not placed in leadership positions. Latin Americans do not expect to be made leaders by us, perhaps in part because they have experience with North American missionaries in their home nations who have marginalized them in some way. At the same time, they know they are educated, experienced, and talented, so they know they can and should be leaders. We keep surprising people when we happily invite them into the process of leading and try to promote them.

We have had some very positive results training couples for leadership from both Latin America and Europe. Each time, they were surprised that we would trust them and put them in charge of people from the United States. It can be disheartening to see how surprised these excellent leaders are when we give authority and leadership to them within our organization. It grieves my heart that they express amazement at being treated as trustworthy equals, but we rejoice that things have been changing in these relationships in recent years. Given that we are brothers and sisters in one family under Christ, this shift toward leadership from around the globe is a positive step.

Finally, leadership modeled after Jesus's approach of serving first provides a framework for building healthy multinational teams. In a serve-first example of Jesus, the leader takes up the towel to do what is necessary for the flourishing of the follower (John 13). How does this work in teams where leadership culture and different assumptions about power and authority between leaders and followers persist?

Leadership that is other-oriented and seeks to serve first has been a challenging but rewarding model for multinational teams. As leaders ask, "How can I best serve this person?" their need to "do it my way" diminishes, and a desire to listen and adapt to others grows. We have not always been successful at serving this way, but in those times when listening first and serving first are guiding our steps, our teams run more smoothly and our life together is enriched by the various cultures present in our multinational team.

## In-Christ Training for "Mission with" Multinational Partners

Teams are challenging for leaders and followers alike. The idea of *team* could be plumbed endlessly for the cultural assumptions it brings to the table. Teams necessarily involve working together, leadership and followership, authority, goal-setting, power, and any number of other factors. In multinational ministry teams, assumptions about God and the nature of ministry impact team dynamics as well.

In the first year or two of on-the-field training, people find themselves between competencies and between identities. Becoming an expat with an intercultural become-part-of-this-new-culture attitude creates a crisis in identity. Coping mechanisms are gone; skills and talents (temporarily) do not apply. We were competent at life and no longer are: How do I shop? How do I ask for a restroom . . . wait, what? You have to *pay* for the bathroom? And so on.

We refer to this identity crisis as deconstruction—an internal change that seems to take place when people really engage in the field and consider it as a long-term option. The process creates a social space in between who I was (pre-deconstruction) and who I will be (post-reconstruction). If we allow the Lord to work, if we remain attentive to and submissive to the movements of the Spirit, the Lord will reconstruct us to be more like Jesus and ready to tackle the work he has for us. If we resist, we end up seeking refuge in the way we were—we escape the in-between space by retreat rather than by going through it.

We have learned, in our years of equipping men and women who bring their unique personal callings to our program, that not everyone is a "fit." For some, the gap in expectations—ours and theirs—was never resolved. For others, the language gap was an issue that turned out to be too great for us to reasonably keep moving forward. In these situations, helping locate other opportunities for our colleagues that are better fits is a way of serving everyone involved. While such separations were painful, both sides also felt a sense of relief. We desire that those who leave will have experienced a sense of being loved in a community of the "body of Christ," even though we were not a good fit as a team. We do not feel that everyone must fit into the team culture we are trying to create: the point of a training team for all our multinational team members is to walk together for a season and see whether this will work!

In our work training new ministers of the gospel from diverse backgrounds, we have ended up focusing on a few key elements of the Christian life to help us get along together. The character of Jesus provides a central focus: Am I reflecting him, or am I merely reflecting my own culture's values? In this rubric, enacted faith and self-sacrificial love end up being central. As I willingly learn to live faithfully and serve others through *self-emptying*, many of the challenges of serving together recede. They continue to exist, but rather than being explosive and drama-laden, they look more like conflict in a healthy family. Indeed, this is what we should expect. Our true identity as the family of God does not preclude conflict but offers a guiding metaphor for how we might operate in life together.

## REFLECTION QUESTIONS

- What role does training play in your preparation for cross-cultural teamwork?
- What biblical metaphors do you employ to give focus to teams and relationships?
- How would you describe the "work of faith" in your team relations?
- What in-Christ interventions do you employ best in your team relations?

# 12

## Unequal Partners, Clumsy Compromise

MATTHEW E. CROSLAND

The Pacific Institute of Languages, Arts and Translation (PILAT) is a joint venture between SIL, a multinational organization of expatriates doing Bible translation in Papua New Guinea, and the Bible Translation Association of Papua New Guinea (BTA), which is composed of Melanesian language speakers and teams. Its primary purpose is to train Melanesian Bible translators to multiply workers to provide Scripture for 316 indigenous languages. My assignment in SIL was to serve as director of PILAT—a *role of stewardship* in the body of Christ to ensure that we achieved our purpose of equipping these national Bible translators and teams. The teaching staff has two full-time Melanesian members, and about 30 to 40 percent of the part-time staff are local Melanesians; the others are expatriate SIL members from Western nations—the United States, Australia, Britain, the Netherlands, and so forth.

## Faith, Love, and Hope: A Case Study of Stewardship[1]

The purpose of this chapter is to describe the critical role of bringing together people from radically different cultural backgrounds—Westerners and Melanesian nationals, in this case—for the purpose of developing a new program planning system to equip national workers for the task of Bible translation in Papua New Guinea. As I have reflected on our journey as unequal partners, I have come to the conclusion that faith, love, and hope were essential components in our success at creating a new planning system and in its acceptance by both SIL and the national organization. This entire process was a work of faith. As I looked at our wicked problem, I realized that God wanted something better for my Melanesian colleagues and that we could create change on their behalf. They too saw the potential for substantive change God had placed in front of them, and we all actively engaged in the work of faith.

Our challenge was to learn together and then create together a new process of training. God had been working in all our hearts to prepare us for this moment. He had created unique bonds between us that made the love he placed in us more evident. Because we had experienced this "God love" for each other, we were keen to work selflessly for the betterment of each other and his kingdom.

The story that follows was possible because we shared the hope in Christ that together we could equip his Melanesian followers to bring Scripture to their own people. It gave us focus for what was at stake and a vision for what we could achieve and what it would mean for communities across Papua New Guinea. Our shared faith allowed us to understand this project not as something for this moment or to make our lives easier or even to allow the language programs to work better. We saw it as ministry, moving not only current participants closer to God but the generations to come as well. This was something God was doing through us for our children and their children by extending this steadfast hope through the generations.

1. This case study is adapted from Crosland, "Language Program Planning."

## Unequal Partners: A Wicked Problem

In practice, SIL has been the primary partner in this relationship. SIL expatriates work in an organizational culture that values equity; thus they see any given partnership as one in which we are all equal, and if we are not, we need to do something about it to ensure that we are on a level playing field.[2] In contrast, Melanesians don't have an expectation that both partners will be completely equal. Melanesians view SIL as the "older brother" in control[3] of the partnership. They would say, "Of course, one partner brings more to the partnership than the other, and that's okay. Doesn't the clan expect more from the older brother than the younger?"

SIL has been the primary partner in this relationship since its inception. The Melanesian director of BTA, Tony Kotauga, has expressed a strong interest in playing a larger role in PILAT and its future, and potentially the older brother may need to become the younger brother. In some ways, this puts SIL into a difficult position, because Kotauga and others have included PILAT in their organizational structure and possibly assumed more ownership of it than they should have. However, this is also an opportunity to take a step back and start to let the national translators assume the primary partner role that they have been working toward since PILAT's inception.

One way that SIL has held power in PILAT is by being the sole partner developing curriculum. This is where we experienced the wicked problem, because SIL has embraced results-based management as the system used to teach language program planning, motivated by donor demands for productivity. As a consequence, PILAT's course for program planning was an intricate technical system that was applied in a systematic way by people who had a very good grasp of the English language (primarily native English speakers).[4] This results-

2. Low power distance / internal locus of control.
3. High power distance / external locus of control framework.
4. This program planning course fit well with the Western cultural practices of monochronic time orientation, linear cognitive processing, production orientation, and low power distance (or internal locus of control).

based program planning course fit well with the Western cultural understandings of time, task, dichotomous thinking, and personal control of one's project and work.

## Bringing Value Conflicts to the Surface—Phase 1

To bring to the surface the value conflicts between the Westerners and the Melanesians, in 2017 I selected a sample of twenty participants from those with strong personal interests in PILAT and designed three card sorts (each card picturing people at work), wrote four vignettes (each an open-ended story in the local context), and conducted follow-up interviews with each person.[5] The three card sorts focused specifically on the values of task orientation vs. relational orientation, dichotomous thinking vs. holistic thinking, and sequential time orientation vs. cyclical time orientation. After I had recorded all the data and processed it for presentation, I reported the patterns of response to the mixed group of participants working on the Melanesian program planning project.

Since the participants were a mixed group, I had anticipated that I might receive pressure from both sides. The first response illustrated this tension: "My initial reservation stemmed from the idea that *time*, in a Western sense, does not seem to exist at all in Papua New Guinean thinking. *Cyclical* to me connotes Eastern/Hindu–type worldviews—incorporating death and life into an eternity of spirals which hopefully end in 'gutpela sindaun'/nirvana. So, in that sense, it does not seem to me that Melanesians think cyclically *with regard to time*." I believe that she was right: time in the Western sense largely does not exist in Melanesia, especially not in village settings. However, what she had set up is a dichotomous view of time—Eastern and Western. This is an extreme oversimplification. There are countless nuances in how people understand and use time. But there were certainly enough significant concerns in her statement to warrant concern on my part.

5. For details, see Crosland, "Language Program Planning," 97–110.

## How to Plan and Organize Translation Work—Phase 2

In 2018 we organized a Melanesian Program Planning and Management course to try to address the value conflict between SIL's Western translation systems—designed over many years by the Western translators, who were the predominant users—and the non-Western mother-tongue translators who are now becoming a large part of the broader translation community and need a system that fits their own cultural framework.

In my role as director of PILAT, I became the bridge leader to mediate between the members of SIL and BTA. My first strategy was to ask Australian Barry Borneman, a veteran of both SIL and BTA, to come and teach a one-week intensive language program planning course that he had redesigned for Australian Aboriginal translators. Borneman's first words in this course were these: "Program planning is about people. It is not about filling in a sheet; it is about our relationship with others." Borneman's approach put people squarely at the center of the process and allowed those from relationally based cultures, like Melanesians, to work from their strength rather than forcing them to work through someone else's cultural framework. While Borneman's one-week course remained Western in sequence and design, his relationship emphasis was a massive step forward.

After Borneman finished teaching this people-centered approach, I led the participants through a second week to review and debrief the detailed progression of his course, asking what we learned and what we should change based on my research about value differences between Melanesians and expatriates (described in detail above). From these debriefing sessions, we created a new program planning course. This was the first attempt to give BTA members an opportunity to influence the structure of a curriculum and the first time that this much emphasis had been put on incorporating Melanesian cultural values into the curriculum. Melanesians have a very relational approach to life. They believe that good production happens because good relationships have been nurtured. Western expatriates believe good relationships are fostered by good production. The second week of processing to develop this course led us all to a clumsy compromise.

## A "Clumsy" Compromise: Time and Production

When the cyclical time factor came up for discussion in the second week, the Melanesian participants were very excited about it. This idea that life operates in cycles and that they have to think in cycles to accommodate the nature of life in Papua New Guinea was completely natural to them. They got excited because they had never seen it presented this way, and it had finally been expressed in a way that made sense to them. After that session, I received an email from the person quoted above that read, "The connection between cyclical thinking and planning resonated with me when one of the participants . . . remarked that accomplishing [translation] tasks could be related to the planting/harvesting calendar, i.e. a particular [translation-related] task could be inserted into an agricultural-task slot. So maybe during yam-planting, everyone would also know that village checks would be part of that slot."

This was a very encouraging email to me, since it was a "clumsy" compromise. The writer of this comment follows a Western, production-oriented approach to the subject: it is about accomplishing "translation tasks." The approach we took in the Melanesian program planning course is that Bible translation work must be integrated into the cyclical nature of life in the village. It is not a "task to be accomplished" or boxes to be ticked that exist outside the flow of normal village life.

We spent a good bit of time looking at all the cultural factors and discussing the challenges and benefits of having these two very different clusters of culture working together. As we talked about the challenges, a Melanesian member began to study the card sort data on "production" very closely. The discussion moved on, and he finally spoke up and said, "I have been looking at these charts for some time now and I have realized that though the Westerners are a number 1 on the top and a number 5 on the bottom and we are a number 5 on the top and a number 1 on the bottom, we both have a number 3 in the same place. Why can't we both move to a number 3 and work together?" What an eloquently simple but profound statement and a push toward "elegant" rather than "clumsy" solutions! At first glance, there seemed to be no reason why both parties should not move to the middle and operate there. In fact, it seemed like a very reasonable request, but there were probably countless reasons why this was not possible. I can imagine that one of the first responses would be that "our systems don't work like that."

The other thing that was striking in this discussion was how interested each group—Western and Melanesian—was in the other's scores. Both groups were surprised by the data; neither had realized just how far apart they were. The participants told numerous stories about their expectation that the other group would operate under their cultural norms and their shock and dismay when it did not.

The participants asked me to include the findings from the card sort and vignette exercises in the document packages they were taking home. They wanted to share the results with other people they were working with, because they thought it would be significant for their cross-cultural interactions in the future. This positive feedback gave me the confidence to present my data to a wider audience and to move forward with the changes that we were creating together.

## One Mission, Two Planning Models

The participants created a distinctively Melanesian program planning model and refined it to cover beginning-to-end program planning and year-by-year planning to guide translators in what is always a long-term process. The Melanesians gave priority to vision and community discussion, stating that vision was critical to motivate people to participate and that community discussions are one of the most important ways that decisions are made locally. If the community believes it has been excluded from the decision-making process or if people feel that their voices have not been heard, there will be no community ownership or support.

The most important difference between the SIL and the Melanesian versions of program planning is the way participants approach the task of planning. The SIL results-based model is sequential: the program proceeds like building blocks being stacked into an elegant structure. The Melanesian approach to planning is cyclical, moving through vision, results, community discussion, planning, activities, and resources in recurring patterns of action. Melanesians found the distinction between short-term and long-term production confusing and unnecessary. They decided to use "the fruits of work" or "the fruits of our labor" to describe what should happen in each cycle of planning.

I encouraged the Melanesians to organize the work of planning in similar recurring patterns, allowing freedom to change things as needed. This kind of planning activity parallels the cyclical thinking and approach to time typical in Melanesian life and work. Finally, the SIL results-based model includes a chart summary to be filled out and followed. In contrast, I instructed our course participants that a pen should never touch the Melanesian summary chart. Rather, the chart should always be filled out with a pencil, because it is a living document that should grow and change with the language program and the needs of the language community.

## A Bridge Organization for "Mission With"

As we have already noted, it is very difficult to come out of one's culture of origin and operate in another way. This is even more true when a person is put into a stressful situation. We try our best to return to our default culture when we are stressed. Team members feel stress when confronted with expectations that are difficult or uncomfortable.

I feel that part of our role at PILAT is to be a bridge between organizations in regard to culture. Most organizations are structured around their members' home culture and foster expectations that things should function according to that culture. This is all very good until the organization moves out of its home culture and into another. Expectations about things like accounting practices, use of time during the workday, and responsibilities to family and friends can change drastically from one culture to another, while the expectations of the organization remain the same. The fact that the people who are responsible for making the final decisions for the organization are generally still in the home culture and do not understand the cultural issues in the new country works to compound the issues.

I believe that in these sorts of situations it is critical to have someone who is a bridge person or, in the case of PILAT, to have a bridge organization. This person or organization understands both cultures well and can help to bring about mutual understanding. People who fill this role can give insight to both sides about cultural cues that they might be missing or potential pitfalls. I think that PILAT has the ability and the responsibility to be this type of organization between SIL, BTA, and outside funding organizations. We have a vested interest in the success of all the parties involved.

I am not sure what this will actually look like, nor do I think it is static enough to write out guidelines. I think it will look different in different situations depending on what is at stake and who the participants are. It is my hope that by collaborating in this way, we can promote unity in the body of Christ and facilitate the furtherance of his kingdom. The underpinning of faith, hope, and love has made this collaboration possible and, in the end, successful. I am very thankful for all the ways that God has worked through this process to bring about the Melanesian program planning course for a future generation of Melanesian translators of Scripture.

## REFLECTION QUESTIONS

- What do you think was the driving force behind SIL's results-based planning model for Bible translation?
- Why is a Western curriculum on any topic not well received in Melanesia?
- What do you see as most creative about Crosland's "meek" leadership, and what did you learn from it?
- What does Crosland mean when he calls PILAT a "bridge" organization?

# 13

## *Koinonia* Teamwork
## in Central Africa

MARTINS ATANDA

Zion World Prayer and Missions is an indigenous Nigerian mission to non-followers of Jesus Christ across Central Africa and beyond. In this chapter, I tell the story of how God led me to establish this mission for the purpose of mobilizing Christian leaders and churches in Nigeria—and across Central Africa—to bring the good news of Jesus Christ to unreached people groups. For the sake of clarity, I have divided the story into three phases of this ministry: (1) mobilizing workers—forming a core team; (2) organizing regional teams—following God's vision; and (3) building international teams—having steadfast hope. Throughout this chapter, I will share the challenges of bringing Christians together from the diverse denominations established by Western missionaries, from diverse tribal backgrounds, and from both Anglophone and Francophone colonial nations. Our focus is *koinonia*, a sacrificial community of faith bringing good news to the unreached in Africa.

## PHASE 1: Mobilizing Workers—Forming a Core Team

In 1995, my responsibility as pastor and canon in the Anglican Church of Sokoto, Nigeria, included teaching theological education by extension and leading the local programs in evangelism and mission. In this role, using materials I had learned to use in theological college, I wrote a training manual for students (professionals in their jobs but serving the church in lay roles) enrolled in our theological education by extension program.

I felt limited by the Anglican leaders as I began to move into mission work. They preferred that I focus on mobilizing people to serve in the local churches, but I sensed the call of God to mobilize people for ministry to nonbelievers. During that time, some Muslims came to our church showing an interest in the gospel. As we rejoiced in their interest and response, we asked, "Why not take the gospel to them?" I decided to leave the Anglican Church to give my time fully to mobilizing individuals for evangelism and church planting.

After separating—with some pain—from the Anglican Church, I formed a board of supporting friends and gathered a handful of Anglican Yoruba men to expand the training program. I refocused on equipping and mobilizing workers for mission, and we did a traveling series of one-week-per-month training conferences in different locations in Nigeria. During this early mobilization phase of ministry, one of our board members asked me, "How can you mobilize others to reach people of other faiths without any experience of your own in this task?" From this challenge, the Spirit moved us, and we began engaging nonbelievers to share the gospel with them.

As our ministries expanded beyond Sokoto, we trained our Yoruba Anglican leaders and new recruits—Hausa, Dakarkari, Gobirawa (Baptists), Igbo, and South South (Pentecostals)—how to do research to learn the dynamics of what was happening in the place to which God was leading us. These men became my "mission core" team for ministry. We visited a town, talked to the leaders, listened to the people, and listened to the Holy Spirit as we prayed for the town. Once we had gathered information, we began praying for direction about how to share Christ. In the power of the Spirit, we rebuked demonic, cultural, and social forces that opposed the gospel—praying through the night.

## The Work of Faith—Prayer, Fasting, New Lands

From that time forward, prayer has been a major focus of our preparation and support ministry. My prayer time and leadership have focused on those who became the "mission core" team of eight to ten men. Every night, we all set apart an hour—during the midnight hour—for prayer *together*, intercession before God for direction and guidance, on our phones or in person. This has been done and is still done throughout all seasons of the year.

In January of each year, we also have a daily fast for twenty-one days. At the end of each day, we have joint prayers in the evening with other supporting believers and members of the ministry, and then we break our fast collectively, as is the practice of Muslims during Ramadan. Every month from February to November, we have three days of fasting and prayer, and again, at the end of the day, we pray together in the evening and then break our fast. In the week that straddles November and December every year, we embark on one week of fasting—for three days we break the fast with food in the evening, but the last two or three days we eat no food but have water alone.

For our apostolic kind of ministry—new fields, new lands—we don't send the younger generation; our mission core leaders are the first to move. We expect that the people with whom we pray consistently will lead the teams that they are shepherding in the same manner, so that prayer overflows into every aspect of our ministry. Only in this way are we able to stand against the attacks of our enemy—the ancient serpent—the devil.

In our ministries to the poor, we face daily challenges of spiritual opposition, evil forces working against us, and evil problems in most of these communities: bloodshed, impoverishment, stealing, and even attacks on missionaries. Every time some person accepts Christ, that person and we face opposition and have problems. We must provide support and resources to help new converts become disciples. When the jihadist movement intensified, we were forced to register with police, to speak with local leaders, and to get permission even before having conversations to exchange ideas.

The work of faith became the most essential of the virtues to us—we have trusted God for every challenge and for every step of the work. Our churches in Nigeria and the nations around were low in finances and didn't have much to give; often we felt alone. But God inspires people from everywhere—the south, east, and west—so we prayed and waited for funds to come. There was nothing else we could do. We worked by faith every time. We didn't reschedule a mobilization conference; we just went. If a motorbike broke down, we pushed it to the location of the training conference; we slept anywhere; we ate when we could find food.

## The Labors of Love—Training, Sharing, Caring

We found that when God led people to us and we gave them the privilege of training—hearing the Word of God, praying together for God's mission, then participating in the work—some responded with commitment and passion. John Babalola's story illustrates this process. Babalola grew up in a Muslim family, and his father is still Muslim. As a motorbike mechanic, he met many Christians in Sokoto, and from those contacts he became a Christian, worshiping in a Baptist church. We invited him to come with us on several mission trips, which finally led him to attend a training conference on mission work. After this experience, he said he wanted to be involved, so I sent him to discuss this with his Baptist pastor.

After he consulted with his pastor, we sent him as a mentee missionary to an unreached Muslim-majority area. One of our staff members, John Edibo, went with new recruits Babalola and Yohana Joseph to this area, helping them interface with a leprosy health center started by German doctors. Using media to preach the gospel—especially the *Jesus Film*—they expressed God's grace to the patients at this health center. Babalola became committed to evangelistic ministry, leading outreach to towns in Kebbi and Zamfara states and then to Niger state, and doing leadership training there. He is now one of our senior leaders in charge of mobilization conferences in Cameroon and Chad. When our ministry began, our primary labor of love was *koinonia*—as a team, we ate together, our meals the same measure for everyone; if someone brought clothing, we shared it with others in need; when one man offered me a car, we sought to meet the needs of all team members with motorcycles—I didn't need much. One team member has always been in charge of accounts, and I have regularly contributed my money to the ministry fund. Nobody was left behind in giving. People just gave out of love and compassion.

When we want to start engagement, we ask, "How is God leading us to open dialogue and to do acts of love within this community?" We have many potential resources—the *Jesus Film*, God's Story (video media), Operation Blessing (food and water), the Christian Broadcasting Network, and locally supplied media; we drill water wells and distribute clothing—guided by local needs and the resources available.

Our strategy has always been to gather people, feed them the Word, and—when possible—also feed them with food that we have brought. I have used my savings to buy food so people can cook. When the Anglican Church gave me a salary, I didn't need it—my father supported me—so I used my salary to help poor pastors and used money from my father to feed people at different conferences, whether youth camp meetings or prayer and mission conferences. We brought what we could; we did not plan, since we had no idea how many people would come, but we bought a cow, bags of rice, sugar, and coffee. Most times, whatever we had in food lasted for the conference. It seems God multiplied our supplies. We didn't take an offering; God provided. We traveled to places with no extra money for gas; when I traveled with my wife, we slept in the car.

### "Testing Our Commitment"—a Wicked Problem of Finance

From 1997, our work advanced with a "mission core" team of ten who came from diverse careers and denominations, and even from tribal areas in Nigeria. We organized free training conferences—mobilizing

people for mission—in six locations across Nigeria. To staff a conference, we had to travel to the location, conduct the training over five
days, and then return home. We typically had no provision for housing, and we used the little money we had for food and transportation.
Our funds were so limited that we usually could afford to send only
one person to lead a training conference. Our money that supported
travel came largely from income obtained by using my car as a taxi
in the city of Sokoto.

On one occasion in 1999, two of our core leaders—one Yoruba
and one South South—traveled together to one location to host a
training conference. They intentionally broke the travel expense rules,
exceeding their expense allotment, so we had no money to fund the
next week's training conference. When they approached me, I said,
"We have no money; you need to find on your own how to solve the
problem you created." One of them asked, "Why don't we charge
money for training? Is it okay?" I said no: "It has been our policy from
the beginning to provide training at no cost to the participants. We
cannot change this policy just because we don't have a budget—we
will wait on the Lord." The Yoruba leader who had asked the question got angry and finally resigned. A few days later, I was surprised
when the South South training partner and an Igbo colleague who
shared an apartment with them also resigned.

To understand these leaders' response to this crisis, it is helpful to
understand the power of belonging to one's group in Nigerian cultures and the shame and loss of face that the Yoruba man felt when
we rejected his proposal to charge tuition. His anger stemmed from
the implication of "blame" for the "problem you created" and shame
about the loss of face among his ministry partners. He felt enough
shame that he resigned from the mission rather than seek help, and
the other two partners in ministry shared in that shame and anger
about our policy on finance.

After this conflict, I was surprised again when some others of our
core mission staff decided to leave the ministry without giving specific
reasons. I thought the work was going to close. But when our auditor
did the year-end audit of our account, he said, "You saved money, you
did more things: the exit of these guys reduced our costs." We have

remained committed to teaching without cost to students, trusting the Lord for our needs at each location. Some of the graduates have brought gifts to us, but we do not charge.

This finance issue was a testing time for us: We passed the test; we didn't have to humanly manage our situation. We continued to walk in faith and to wait on the Lord to supply our needs. I wasn't happy that these men left, and I thought they would be able to overcome the crisis of that moment; how they left was painful. As of 2020, only two of the original ten core members remain with me in ministry. God—leading me to use second- and third-generation leaders—has expanded this ministry to its present scope.

## God's Gift of Funding

As illustrated in the conflict crisis described above, funding has always been precarious but essential for moving forward. From the beginning of our ministry, we invited believers who were flourishing in business to attend prayer programs for these communities. At these meetings, we challenged them to set aside a percentage of their profits for mission in Nigeria. Many began the practice of sending a monthly donation designated to support evangelism in cities in Nigeria.

Anthony Achebe was one of those early donor-partners in 2000. Trained as a lawyer, he was working in a bank that was in crisis, at the brink of closure. When he was invited to our fellowship meeting, he was moved by the Holy Spirit to commit his work and funds to God's mission to the unreached in Nigeria. In the months that followed, God intervened, saved the bank, and gave Achebe the inspiration to promote our funding efforts—Project Cities of God. Achebe has testified, "I raised that organization to support Zion World Prayer and Missions, dedicated to God to support mission. I work on the secular side, then raise money from people in secular employment to support the missions project. When we do things based upon God's inspiration—follow the leading of the Spirit—these conflicts fade."

In addition to these supporters, we began operating farms to generate funds, and we used my car as a taxi to make money to fund the work. God blessed these businesses and increased our supporting network from this time forward. We have also received funding from overseas in the form of single gifts for specific projects and some recurring gifts for general support for the mission work.

## PHASE 2: Organizing Regional Teams—Following God's Vision

In 2001 my wife was invited to serve as a volunteer to help the Evangelism and Missions Commission of the Association of Evangelicals in Africa—a subset of the World Evangelical Alliance—to organize a conference on mission for the Central African Republic, Cameroon, Chad, and Sudan. I was also asked to teach on small groups. At this conference I was astonished to learn that a Christian pastor had become a Muslim because he lacked food. I also noticed a man attending all the sessions wearing the same jacket every day. I wondered, Is this a uniform, or is it the only coat he has? So I asked. He told me it was the only coat he had. As I was praying over that experience, the Holy Spirit moved me to sacrifice what I had, so I gave him some of the clothing I had brought with me.

During this conference—while in prayer—I fell into a trance. A giant appeared to me—the appearance of evil. When he approached me, I saw him wearing three caps, one on top of the other. The top cap was white, and I thought, With a white cap, he can't be evil; he must be good. When I reached out and grabbed the cap, it was a disguise: hypocrisy, Christians ashamed of the gospel. I saw people watching from afar begin to hail and cheer. Then I understood: all across French-speaking Africa, I was seeing fear of the shame of sacrificial living to share the gospel with rival people and communities.

Reaching again for the giant's cap, I grabbed it—a red one—and again people from afar hailed and cheered. This cap represented fighting and bloodshed, and I realized that Côte d'Ivoire, Rwanda, Congo, the Central African Republic, Senegal, Chad, and most of the African French-speaking countries were filled with fighting and bloodshed. Fighting is all about groups—our group against your group, our honor against your honor, and your shame to avenge our shame. Finally, I reached out to grab the third and last cap, a black one, and I heard in the Spirit "death": human lives, human visions, human hope—dead all across Francophone Africa.

Then I heard the Spirit say, "Go to these lands; teach my Word; teach people to overcome the desire for bloodshed; teach people to seek transformation; teach them business; share with them your food, clothing, shoes, and resources for well-being; pray for the ending of fighting and wars."

### The Prayer Tours to Mobilize Francophone Teams

Prompted by this vision and prayerful reflection, I began planning the first of what have become mobilization and equipping prayer tours. Using the ancient biblical skills—song, word, worship, prayer, sacrifice, and service—each prayer conference included the following:

- prophetic prayers for the land and people
- teachings on community transformation—live simply that others may live
- teaching businesspeople to create wealth to finance the spread of the gospel
- presentation of ministry materials—books, tapes, Bibles—to participants
- gifts of food, clothing, and shoes to encourage missionaries, pastors, and the people

We sang, worshiped, and taught in the daytime and engaged in spiritual warfare through prayers at night. We prayed Scripture over particular territories, then we moved to prayer on site in each local context. The Lord is faithful: during this first tour, people experienced no harm, and God's presence and prayers were ever active with them.

We—the core team—then launched a series of prayer conferences in 2003 and 2004 across Francophone Africa to raise up regional teams and recruit new workers to share the gospel. From that time to now, God has raised up people in Nigeria and in all the surrounding nations to supply all our funding needs for going to these African nations. God has called the churches to repentance and has called God's people to move out in faith to their neighbors with the gospel of Christ crucified, carrying gifts of compassion and the hope of salvation and abundant life in Jesus Christ.

What happened from these training conferences? We sought to multiply teams in every area where God moved people to respond. After a person completed the training twice, like John Babalola, we encouraged this person to go out and take part in the mission activities with one of the core mission staff and begin to take a leadership role in mission and ministry. People from many different denominations attended our conferences. We became popular for building the capacity of the body of Christ for ministry, starting new teams in every area, without boasting of one superior denomination. We saw the advancement of the gospel in different communities. The training empowered people to serve with little or no funding.

In recruiting young believers to the ministry, *we de-emphasize tribe and denomination.* We ask each person, "Where is God leading you to work?" We present the picture of our outreach, the program of God for Africa, a global vision! We ask, "Where is God leading you, and how is God gifting you to serve this global vision?" When people embrace this vision, the fear of a local setting and of group opposition is diminished, and the hunger for honor and the fear of shame is refocused toward the mission of God.

God expanded our commitment through the vision of the giant—Francophone Africa—in 2001, so that by 2020, we and our ministry partners—regional mobilization teams—had engaged the unreached and unengaged people groups in Nigeria, Burkina Faso, and across Francophone Africa. The goal that drives us is to reach more of the 90 unreached people groups in Nigeria and to mobilize others across Africa to engage the 960 remaining unreached groups.

## PHASE 3: Building International Teams—Having Steadfast Hope

Because of the opposition to the gospel across Francophone Africa, we (Nigerians) partnered with Christian immigrants to these nations to form international teams. These immigrants from Benin and Nigeria lived and worked in Niger or Mali, but as Christians they had no strategy for reaching the local Zjerma people. It was easier to reach other foreign immigrants than to reach the local Zjerma.

The Zjerma people are the most prominent unreached ethnic group from Niger to Mali in North Africa (the French call them Taureg). Our prophetic prayer across Niger and Mali focused on these people. In many countries, Christianity is a threat—a political and cultural threat. Even the locals across the region say that if you become a Christian, you may marry only one wife and you can't lie anymore, which is very inconvenient. Christianity doesn't allow you to deceive—yes must be yes, no must be no—and deception is essential to avoid shame and to protect one's group and personal honor. If you become a Christian, you are not behaving like an average tribal person. Education is open to you. Christianity liberates you, and you even have a picture of eternal life. We Christians embrace these things, but they are a threat to these locals in their everyday life habits.

So, in hope of penetrating the opposition of the Zjerma, in 2005 we equipped and mobilized several men from the Bahare tribe of Niger, men recognized by the multiple marks—intentional scarring—on their faces, similar to the Gobirawa in Niger. These men attended our mobilization conference and said they were interested in mission. Since they were from Niger, knew the country, and seemed ready and able to reach the Zjerma, we sent them out. We needed people who could drink camels' milk and sleep on the roof at night, and who understood the local lifestyle of the Zjerma.

To equip them, we provided accommodation, food, and training until they were ready to go out on mission. After they finished our orientation, we gave them money and cycles, and we sent them out—first to the Kamba in Nigeria, then to the Malanville in Benin, and then to the Zjerma in the Republic of Niger. We provided for each a monthly allowance to help them start, and we were regularly praying for and supporting them.

After about a year, these missionaries just disappeared into thin air. We heard from another Bahare—a pastor with us among the Gobirawa—that he saw one of these Bahare in another location, where he had started a church. We wondered why, despite all our gifts and support, this man gave no report, no update on the fruits of his ministry. We later found that the man is pastoring Bahares who are believers, but he has not engaged any communities of the unreached Zjerma.

We concluded that the doors to the Zjerma were locked, so we took a step back from their territory and tried to build relationships with immigrant Christians in Niger, Mali, Cameroon, and Chad. Every support platform we built to penetrate the Muslim people groups, the devil knocked down—one after another.

## Opposition, Violence—Times of Despair

Throughout the years, we have experienced opposition wherever we go, even among believers in local churches. In the border town of Yaguoa on the Chad side of the Chari River, I challenged pastors to pray for the end of the periodic wars among their people. One of the old men stood up on the platform where the pastors were seated together, and he said, "Young boy, how old are you? For the past forty years, I have seen war all of my life; you don't know what you are talking about." As the Spirit reveals "hypocrisy" in God's vision, so many—like this man—confess to be Christian, but they question God's Word and do not trust God to work through them to change their nations. Are they ashamed of the gospel? Do they fear shame from rivals?

We also continue to see bloodshed—violence perpetuated by nations, governments, and insurgents such as Boko Haram. In 2011, while we were traveling to meet our conference tour schedule in Côte d'Ivoire, the police and army stopped our van at a roadblock and kept eight of us in prison for one night. The next day they released us but commanded that we depart in the opposite direction. They closed churches; they didn't want prayer. People want to shed blood. Why? Power-seeking and political tensions are destroying the governments and the people of these nations and bringing others to power. And death is everywhere in these nations, destroying pagans, Christians, and Muslims alike.

## "Mission with Partners"—Steadfast Hope

But in all of this, God brings to us people who love him and who give us hope. One bicultural woman named Safiatou—whose father is Zjerma and whose mother is Fulani—married Frank, a Nigerian living in Niger. We first met Safiatou when she attended our annual prayer conference in Niamey, Niger, in 2003 and—moved by the Holy Spirit to follow Jesus—she asked me for a connection to follow the vision we had shared. We went to Niger to preach to believers, and she—fluent in French—was my translator. Subsequently, Safiatou and Frank invited me to baptize them in the River Niger on the Niger side as a witness to local people. Years after their baptism, they started a church and a secular school for children.

After the disappointment of the Bahare evangelists, Safiatou and Frank encouraged me by starting this local indigenous church. Since then, Safiatou has been busy touring countries in the region and mobilizing women to pray (Wailing Women). Each year when we returned to these countries, she traveled with our core team to Senegal, Mali, Burkina Faso, Malta—even to Geneva, Switzerland.

About four years ago, God began to open doors across Francophone Africa after Safiatou joined our core team as the French translator, enabling us to engage in these French-language contexts through her readiness to travel and translate. What we thought were closed doors, God has gone beyond our expectations to open, giving us fresh contacts. Learning from past teachings and experiences, we are better equipped to teach men and women now, and we have gained further insights on how to build new relationships. God has used us to meet with many new people. Others that we had met before are picking up the baton. These men and women are reaching tribal people by themselves.

Over the twenty-five years of our mission of mobilization, we have equipped disciples and developed three different spheres of teamwork and support: mission core, regional mobilization, and international mobilization. All teams have at least two members, and more often they have three to six persons to ensure companionship and fellowship and to fight against isolation, which can quickly undermine ministry to unreached people groups.

Among these teams we have mobilized multitribal participants—Hausa people, Fulani nomadic people, Dukawa, and Kemberi, Kamukawa, Bahare, Gobirawa, and Tuareg tribes in the Republic of Niger. We are planning conferences in 2021 in Sudan, Cameroon, Chad, Mauritania, and Senegal to recruit and mobilize Christian workers to target and adopt these 960 unreached groups. The majority of these groups are in Sudan and Chad.

The Spirit is breathing new life into seeds that we had sown, which were seemingly unfruitful but are now producing fruit. For example, a handful of Mali converts, who came to us in Benin, are now partnering to reach other people in Mali and moving into other countries. Village churches in some rural areas of Mali have started missions in other villages, and two years ago they reached beyond to a few villages in the desert toward Senegal. Churches are growing, and the locals by themselves are reaching their peoples and other tribes.

But our investment has not come to full term, has not produced the kind of fruit among the poor, war-torn, and oppressed that we wanted. And we realize that for many who went, the initial motive was short of fulfilling the purpose of evangelizing the unreached. But we look back and there are no regrets. Even though the churches planted seem few, the seeds planted are sure to grow and reproduce. We rejoice in the partners who have accepted the mobilization challenge, and our hope is in the Lord Jesus Christ, ruler of heaven and earth!

## REFLECTION QUESTIONS

- What about this case study of "mission with" surprises you? Why?
- Given that there are so many languages, cultures, and denominations in Central Africa, what do you think about Atanda's

advice: "*We de-emphasize tribe and denomination.* We ask each person, 'Where is God leading you to work?'"

- How do the "in the world" cultures of Central Africa shape the churches that are planted within them? How does your culture shape your church?
- What is the role of prayer for this mission, and what evidence do you see in the story of God's response?

# PART 4

# Leadership Challenge, Steadfast Hope

The previous chapters shared five stories of leaders on a journey toward unity and mission in spite of the wicked problem of conflicted expectations among team members. In part 4, we consider these stories together to understand the larger in-Christ essentials for multinational teamwork.

Chapter 14 explores how these leaders have used authority and power. All of these leaders discovered that even a commitment to in-Christ metaphors—shepherd, servant, steward—while helpful, could be distorted by default habits and loyalty to a way of life. Leaders and members struggled at times with a default habit of power striving—redeemed only when leaders and team members accepted their utter dependence upon Jesus Christ. Listening to the leading of the Holy Spirit, Scripture, and the team members, these leaders did not try to change the values of the people with whom they worked but rather employed the work of faith and the labor of love to move their team toward unity in Christ.

Chapter 15 reflects on the meaning of the five stories analyzed for cross-cultural teamwork in view of the four goals set forth in the preface—identify wicked problems, discern the biblical essentials, respond "in Christ" to deceptions, and provide case studies. Following the theme of steadfast hope, the chapter reviews the practices of these leaders to discern how they—through serving and suffering with one another in Christ—frame possible futures to work effectively as cross-cultural, multinational teams.

# 14

||||||||||||||||||||||||||||||||||||||||||||||||||||||||||||||||||||||||||||||||||||||||||||||||||||||||||||||||||||

# The Leadership Challenge
of Wicked Problems

SHERWOOD G. LINGENFELTER

Chapters 10 through 13 in this book provide evidence of four distinct styles of leadership used by leaders seeking to resolve wicked problems within their distinctive "households of faith." Each of the respective mission organizations has a governance structure different from that of the others, and each "household" that our respective leaders oversee is formed with reference to both the organization and its very diverse membership. The challenge, then, for these leaders is to navigate the expectations and requirements of their sponsoring organizations and the expectations and requirements of the members of their household of faith.

In this chapter, I review, compare, and contrast how each of these leaders navigates these differences in Christ in order to (1) mobilize their people to be people of God, (2) live and work in a household of faith, and (3) engage in the work of faith, the labor of love, and steadfast hope of advancing the mission of God. But before we consider these cases, I will briefly discuss issues of power and leadership "in the world."

## Soft Power, Redeemed Power, Meek Leaders

In her case study in chapter 4, Julie reports how a secular researcher, Keith Grint, argues that in wicked problems the only recourse for leaders is to apply "soft power" to "ask the right questions rather than provide the right answers because the answers may not be self-evident and will require a collaborative process to make any kind of progress."[1] The nature of soft power is to engage the emotional and habit-formed behaviors of participants, mediating differences among followers through face-to-face work so that they are motivated to listen to one another and to compromise. However, the concept of "soft power" doesn't take into account the deeper spiritual power that we have in Christ, which enables us to practice what we have called in this book the *labor of love*. Further, our emotions war against us, leading us to believe that our way is the "right" way—and once we are convinced that we are right, we feel justified about coercing others to follow us, and even abusing them if they do not agree or follow.

Figure 14.1 is an adaptation of the five ways of life (see fig. 4.1) that Julie used to interpret the power struggles within her team. The picture presents to us four frames of leadership—the authority frame, the corporate frame, the consensus frame, and the influence frame—which are the structural prototypes of social authority available to people in the world. The authority and influence frames are common where people (team members) value individualism or are isolated and powerless in a bureaucracy, deferring to authority without the commitment to or support of a group. The corporate and consensus frames are common where people define their identity by membership within groups (for example, "I am Presbyterian") and have strong commitments to work together within the group. Right in the center of figure 14.1 we see "I AM—JESUS" overlapping the other four images, breaking their circles, which signifies how Jesus is the only

1. Grint, "Problems, Problems, Problems," 1473.

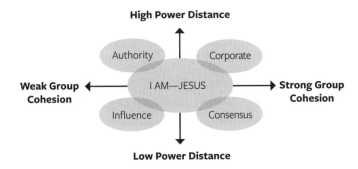

**Figure 14.1** Prototype social frames of leadership

power able to penetrate and transform these "in the world" frames of leadership through his presence in us and our obedience to him.

David Bremner, my colleague in mission, argues appropriately that "Jesus is shepherd, servant and steward all at the same time. . . . The three images are three views of the same picture"—that is, of Jesus.[2] Figure 14.1 illustrates how Jesus is the power that may, at the invitation of the participants in a group, penetrate and transform all social frames of authority and leadership. Our challenge is to understand how this presence of Jesus may be understood and applied in these different frames. As human beings, we live with radically different languages and cultures, most of which do not include sheep or shepherds and many of which have no "servants" or "stewards." We often struggle to follow Jesus in even the smallest things, and these images are complex and challenge us deeply in our quest to follow him.

Further, the Scriptures reveal to us that even these metaphors are often misunderstood and inadequate to redirect humans who seek power in leadership. In every case, the Scriptures show the dark side of each of these images. So the question for me in this chapter is this: How did our contributing authors understand each of these metaphors in their practice of ministry, and how did they practice what they understood each to mean in their leadership challenge?

But first we must examine how Scripture describes the distortions of these metaphors in the world. In figure 14.2, each metaphor—apostle,

2. Bremner, *Images of Leadership*, 1–2.

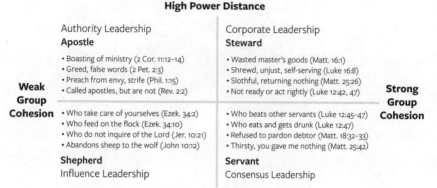

**Figure 14.2** Biblical images of leadership—the dark side

shepherd, servant, steward—appears within the frame that best illustrates the kind of human social authority implied in that metaphor. Then alongside the metaphor I have listed passages of Scripture that show how people who claim those roles use the powers of their position to distort and destroy what God has intended for good. "In the world" apostles are boastful and greedy and preach false words out of envy and strife. "In the world" stewards are wasteful, shrewd, unjust, and self-serving, and they return nothing to their boss or to their household or organization. Unfaithful servants beat other servants in their group, eat and get drunk with the crowd, refuse to pardon even when they are pardoned, and care nothing about those in need around them. The hired-hand shepherd in John and the "priest, prophet, and king" shepherds in Ezekiel abandon the sheep, take care only of themselves, and do not inquire of the Lord. In brief, adopting any one of these images will not serve us apart from our relationship with Christ; conformity to the world destroys each image.

Anita Koeshall, a missionary and scholar researching leadership in the church, contrasts the *power striving* tendencies of humans, which is what we see in figure 14.1, with what she terms "redeemed power." Authority and power are ever present in every human community, regardless of framing around group or varying hierarchies of power. Such power is "redeemed" only when members of a community

recognize first their utter dependence on Jesus Christ and then recognize "the Spirit's gifts in individual members and [create] space
for them to develop their gifts and to function in service to others. Redeemed power is embodied in redeemed agents investing in
a lifestyle of self-emptying for the sake of others."[3] Koeshall's definition reflects beautifully what Paul describes in Ephesians 4 and
5—members of the body of Christ, recipients of the grace and gifts
of Christ, equipped for service and living in mutual submission to
one another to do works of service "until we all reach unity in the
faith and in the knowledge of the Son of God and become mature,
attaining to the whole measure of the fullness of Christ" (Eph. 4:13).

Koeshall elaborates further how redeemed power engages structures in society: the four structural frames (see fig. 14.1) become fluid,[4]
liquid rather than rigid, driven by gift-based authority and power,
resembling how the human body works in all its parts. The key to
this fluid structure is that all parts grant authority to the persons
gifted for the task at hand. The McLeans (in chap. 11) gave a simple
illustration of this: One of their members had the qualifying visa for
a business start-up; the McLeans—the team leaders—granted authority to this new member to lead the team for this business start-up,
and the McLeans gave their house and resources to support, work
under, and work with this team member. They practiced "redeemed
power" on more than one occasion—a leader submitted to a team
member gifted for business or to one gifted for high-risk evangelism.
On such teams, authority moves to the persons gifted by the Spirit
for the task at hand.

By adopting the posture of mission from a position of weakness,
we acknowledge that Jesus is Lord and we are *his servants*. When we
imitate Jesus, we remember his words: "I am meek and lowly in heart"
(Matt. 11:29 KJV). Like a horse in harness,[5] his power is harnessed,
under the complete control of his Father, and he always does the will
of his Father. We resist the deception of Satan to take control and to

3. Koeshall, "Navigating Power," 76.
4. Koeshall, "Navigating Power," 76–77.
5. In early modern English, horse handlers talked about "meeking a horse," or
getting it under control.

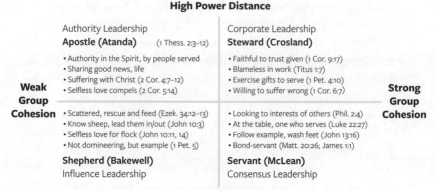

**Figure 14.3** Images of leadership—following Jesus "in the world"

dominate others in the body of Christ. We recognize the marvelous gifts of grace given to members of our teams, and we empower all to exercise their gifts in dynamic collaboration with other members of the body. In step with Ephesians 4:16, leaders accept the profound truth that "the role of the ministry leader is not 'head,' but rather 'supporting ligament,' and the work is not about the performance of the leader or of the body, but about Christ."[6]

In concluding this chapter, I will review the cases of the contributing authors to illustrate how these authors, who have embraced and implemented one or more of these images of leadership in the face of wicked problems, have surrendered their "in the world" social positions and power to others, sharing with them the authority and responsibility of service together in Christ (see fig. 14.3).

## Influence or Shepherd? (Penny Bakewell)

We find Penny Bakewell in chapter 10 facing a challenge as a newly appointed leader regarding how to implement the delegated authority she has as director of SIM Ghana with a leadership team of eight members from four nations—Canada, the United Kingdom, South

6. Lingenfelter, *Leadership in the Way of the Cross*, 107.

Korea, and North East India—who are scattered in several different regions of Ghana, leading smaller ministry teams in these diverse locations. In her first year as leader, she calls the team to gather for meetings in Accra three or four times to discuss issues that affect each of their ministries and require collaboration in order for them to move forward in meaningful ways. Between meetings, the team members communicate with her and one another by email and other media.

Bakewell defined "silence" by these team members as a wicked problem. Why? Because silence isolated her, denying her access to the minds and ideas of her team in a way that made shared leadership impossible. As director, she could have just delegated responsibilities and demanded that people do the work, but that would have been top-down leadership, not "shared" leadership—the pattern preferred by her leaders in SIM. Given the metaphors of shepherd, servant, and steward around which to model her leadership,[7] she chose the shepherd as the metaphor appropriate for her problem and interpreted authority and practice accordingly (see fig. 14.3).

Bakewell understood that her leaders were scattered and working alone without support and care. She discovered early that she did not know them and understood that unless she knew them, she could not lead them. Following Bremner, who is her leadership mentor, she discerned from John 10 that the shepherd is one who "pours out . . . selfless love for their followers" and seeks to enable followers to engage in ways that lead to growth and fruitfulness in their ministry.[8] Bakewell's phrase "don't assume you know; know you know" is her commitment to a labor of love to discover who her team members are and how best to lead them into fruitful participation in and contribution to the total ministry of SIM Ghana.

From the team's point of view, Bakewell is a colleague who has been given authority to lead them, but their charge is to collaborate with her in this process. Yet, as individuals, some are reluctant to speak for reasons other than her role. Some see Bakewell as an equal (the influence frame in fig. 14.1) with whom they share authority.

7. Bremner, *Images of Leadership*.
8. Bremner, *Images of Leadership*, 14–15.

Others see her as director (the corporate frame) with high authority and power. While Bakewell does not use this language, she wants the team to become a "household of faith," willing to participate with her in conversations that lead all the members forward in God's mission for them in Ghana. Her leadership challenge is how to bring these very contrasting viewpoints together to form a household of faith. When she wrote chapter 10, the growth of her team was still in process. As new members continue to be added, the complexity of shared leadership becomes increasingly challenging. However, by taking the role of shepherd, she has found that this work—"knowing" her colleagues—has given her a personal authority and influence to invite them to participate in a household of faith, within which each is valued and empowered for the work of mission.

## Consensus or Servant? (Robert and Elizabeth McLean)

Robert and Elizabeth McLean work in a very different time frame and spatial context. They began as field evangelists in Central Asia and after a term of service were appointed in an organization that follows the corporate style of leadership as directors of training for new missionaries to be deployed in Central Asia for ministries of church planting and discipleship. Challenged by Global Pentecostal Mission to "die to self" and model this for others, they launched an intensive training program in 2012; the training ranges from one to three years. Over the next seven years, they welcomed new missionaries from a global association of Pentecostal churches in North America, Central and South America, Europe, and Asia—all of whom brought their national language and local culture of church and leadership. In order to begin the practice of teamwork and ministry, all studied in English while learning the language of the nation in which they were preparing to serve.

The leadership challenge for the McLeans was and is to encourage team members to let go of the cultural and personal baggage accompanying them that threatens to undermine their efforts to become a household of faith. For Latin Americans, this implies relinquishing authority and control over their ministries (the authority or corporate frames, fig. 14.1) and assuming positions of collaboration and sharing. On the other hand, North Americans—who brought more egalitarian views to teamwork (the influence frame)—perhaps found it challenging to recognize the authority of their senior members.

The McLeans have chosen to define their leadership using the biblical metaphor of servant (see fig. 14.3), as exemplified by Jesus in John 13 taking up the basin and towel to wash his disciples' feet. They embraced a personal and spiritual identity as "bond-servants"—characterized by humility, rejecting self-ambition, and dedicated to the good of their followers.[9] They valued close personal relationships and saw teamwork as sharing mutually in ways that will build up the whole body of the team. While they recognized that they have authority as senior members, they saw the distance between themselves and their members as very small. Their work of faith and labor of love for their satellite teams is collaborative and consensus oriented, working toward an end in which members love one another as brothers and sisters in Christ and serve together as a household of faith.

### Corporate or Steward? (Matthew Crosland)

Matthew Crosland clearly operates within the context of a corporate organization. The SIL branch in Papua New Guinea embodies that corporate structure, made up of self-supporting members who elect their branch director and executive committee. This structure divides corporate responsibility among many, delineating distinct roles for leading and following within the organization. Crosland's position in SIL-PNG is director of SIL training and principal of the institute in which Melanesians are trained to serve as Bible translators. Each of these corporate roles gives Crosland authority to organize and set the direction for particular areas of his responsibility. With reference to the training program, he has oversight of the curriculum. With reference to the training institute, he is responsible to recruit teachers and manage the operation of the school. In Crosland's situation,

9. Bremner, *Images of Leadership*, 24.

the curricular change that he imagined for Melanesians could not possibly be accomplished without the support of his SIL colleagues.

So Crosland's wicked problem and leadership challenge was to bring together the radically different ways of thinking among his colleagues and the Melanesians in training for Bible translation. He knew that the existing program planning course failed in that task. Further, the Melanesian members represented many different tribal groups that had various ideas about leadership style and working relationships. Over a period of three years, Crosland committed to keep both groups working together, build a curriculum, and deliver a training program to Melanesians.

Crosland did not use a biblical metaphor to describe his work, but his case study shows him using "soft" and "redeemed" power in his role as manager or "steward" of a household of faith (see fig. 14.3).[10] That household had older brothers (consensus frame) and younger brothers (influence and corporate frames), and they disagreed about how to get the job done. Crosland treasured the trust that SIL members had in him, and—drawing on a decade of relationships with Melanesian believers—he committed to *serving* both the elder and the younger brothers as a faithful *steward* of God's grace (1 Pet. 4:10). Crosland's labor of love included deep listening to both the elder and younger brothers, and he accepted their challenges, even acknowledging when he was wrong. He led them to understand one another and then guided them to a shared solution for training Melanesians. As a steward of God's grace, he sought to be blameless and faithful to God's purposes—increasing workers for the harvest of the translation of Scripture.

## Authority or Apostle? (Martins Atanda)

We find Martins Atanda in chapter 13 reporting God's faithfulness during twenty-five years of ministry that began when God called Atanda to leave his salaried job as canon in the Anglican Church of Nigeria and take an apostolic role in the founding of a new mission.

10. Bremner, *Images of Leadership*, 31.

Leaving the corporate structure of the Anglican Communion, he began as a shepherd, inviting others of like mind and spirit to join him and create a new mission to reach the unreached peoples in West and Central Africa. One of his disciples, Pastor John Olabode, describes Atanda's work in this way:

> Apostle Martins Atanda is a very passionate believer of possibilities. The regions he invaded were almost impossible places to go, and to some he went during the time of African crisis. He traveled to some of these places despite the dangers and difficulties of the place. I remember one of those days, there was crisis . . . and we told him to postpone the meeting, he said no, that he has given his word and will be there, so he went.
>
> Apostle Martins trained a lot of people like myself. The goal of the ministry is to raise and release men into their various visions. Some may fulfil their vision within the same ministry while others will be released to do so outside the ministry. The ministry has different arms and part of that arm is the church (called Kings Assembly) in the town where I pastor. He founded the church in 1996 and the church has become a cutting edge in the North West of Nigeria. The Apostle of Zion as we popularly call him has fathered many sons and daughters into ministry and when your sons grow up, they will leave to start up their own families while some will stay to take care of the father's labor; so we stayed and some have left.[11]

Atanda's authority has been given to him by the Holy Spirit who called him and by those who have followed him in this ministry. His teammates are the most diverse of all those covered in this book. As this mission grew, the membership shifted from Yoruba and Anglican to interdenominational and new-believer movements to reach the unreached. As Atanda used prayer conferences as the means for bringing people together, God called many attending to join Atanda to reach the unreached, and Atanda actually led them out in their first experiences of ministry (see fig. 14.3).

As Olabode reports, Atanda sought to follow Jesus into the most impossible places, going first and calling his flock to follow him.

11. John Olabode, email correspondence with Sherwood G. Lingenfelter, February 1, 2021.

Atanda taught them to pray, to share the gospel, and to share whatever they had to eat and wear with those to whom they preached. He was a shepherd leading his flock and a servant giving out of his own resources and inviting others to give, to help one another, and to bless those to whom they shared the love of Jesus Christ. Atanda set the example for how resources should be used (acting as a steward), giving sacrificially of his own resources and modeling the same for those who followed him (see fig. 14.3).

In Central Africa, two patterns of leadership are common among unreached people groups: hierarchical clan communities with chief and elder rule (corporate frame) and egalitarian, kinship-ordered communities with elder rule (consensus frame). Tribal groups like the Fulani move as families in continuous migration across the grasslands of Central and North Africa. Their family groups are small, and elders provide direction for each group. Other groups, such as the Hausa, live in towns and work collaboratively under the direction of chiefs and subchiefs. Governments (authority frame) in these regions and states are organized around the most powerful, dominant groups (corporate frame) in that region.

In the course of twenty-five years of ministry, Zion World Prayer and Missions evolved from one core team of ten members into a core team with members from several nations, teams of leaders for each nation or region, and smaller teams spread across the nations of Central Africa. Each team has diverse members with diverse gifts (Eph. 4:12), and decision-making is dispersed among the teams but centered in the apostolic vision and prayer focus of the mission. Atanda's journey brought many wicked problems to the surface—rebellion over finances, Bahare evangelists who disappeared, support platforms knocked down, and individuals and pairs who fell away. In spite of all opposition, Atanda has sought to be shepherd, servant, and steward—a modern-day apostle following and suffering with Jesus—to fulfill God's call in his life to lead Christians in Nigeria and to reach the unreached peoples in Anglophone and Francophone Africa.

Atanda relied on new converts from these diverse populations, teaching them his strategy of loving their neighbors by meeting a specific area of need, sharing with them "redeemed power" and a new way of living in Christ. In each nation and region, Atanda has—through prayer—led the formation of households of faith within which the mission expands. Each regional household has at least two members of Atanda's core team who pray and minister with those who follow locally. New believers follow those who have brought the gospel to them, even as those "sent ones" have followed Atanda. Along the way, churches are planted, and pastors such as Olabode settle in to care for the local flock.

## Old Things Pass Away; All Things Are Made New in Christ

In spite of the wicked problems they illustrate, the five case studies of cross-cultural teamwork in this book present very good news. After two years of struggle, Julie's colleagues in the Southeast Asia Team finally agreed to a "clumsy solution" for working together over the next several years. Bakewell convinced Christians from four nations to work together in unity to lead smaller households of faith for mission in the nation of Ghana. The McLeans have equipped teams of North Americans, Latin Americans, and Europeans to become households of faith working together in unity for the sake of the gospel in Central Asia. Matthew Crosland framed a "clumsy solution" that enabled SIL members from at least eight nations to work with Melanesians for the purpose of Bible translation. Martins Atanda has mobilized followers of Jesus in Francophone and Anglophone African nations, regardless of tribe, language, and denomination, to respond to God's call for prayer and witness to the nonbelievers throughout those nations. It is possible to unite as one church—the body of Christ—when we're willing to suffer to bring the gospel to the unreached.

As we reflect on these five case studies, it is clear that each of these leaders—the writers of these chapters—was working in a situation where cultural differences were so great that they could not use the structures familiar to them from their home churches and nations of origin. Each listened to and learned from the people with whom they worked, and then, under the leading of the Holy Spirit and the wisdom of Scripture, followed Jesus to discover a new way of leading in Christ. In each case, they did not try to change the cultures of the people with whom they worked. Rather, they engaged them in a work of faith to surrender something of their past at the cross with Jesus, and, through the labor of love, invited them into new relationships of serving one another. As members of these teams learned together within the context of their ministries, they were set free from some of the bondage of their past cultures and stepped into a new set of values and relationships that were unique to their teamwork in Christ. The reader can test these leaders' faithfulness by comparing their leadership to the biblical images summarized in figure 14.3. None of these leaders is perfect, but each sought to follow Jesus rather than the pattern of leadership typical of leaders within their world of work and faith.

The argument of this book has been that all effective cross-cultural teamwork must proceed on the basis of our relationship with Christ. Old things must indeed pass away, and all things must become new in Christ (1 Cor. 5:17). Individuals carry many of the "old things" of family and culture with them to their new calling in Christ Jesus. But many, if not most, of those old ways are limiting and constraining. When we rely on the way of the past and live on the basis of our experiences and what we believe to be right, we inevitably cause suffering for ourselves and for others. Our power is not in being "right" but rather in stepping out in faith, doing the labor of love, and believing that hope and perseverance in Christ will lead us to that which God has intended.

## REFLECTION QUESTIONS

- How are "soft power" and "redeemed power" different?
- What is the importance of understanding that Jesus is shepherd, servant, and steward—one person, one Lord, of one essence for us?

- Share with someone how the Spirit has used one or more of these metaphors to challenge your leadership frame in your life and ministry.
- What circumstances might lead you to consider investigating another scriptural metaphor discussed in the chapter and seek to apply it in your leadership?

# 15

|||||||||||||||||||||||||||||||||||||||||||||||||||||||||||||||||||||||||||||||||||||||||||||||||

# "Mission with"—Steadfast Hope

SHERWOOD G. LINGENFELTER

In the preface to this book, we set forth four goals to guide us in our quest to address the substantive issues that teams encounter when their members come together from very diverse national and cultural backgrounds to work for the mission of God. The purpose of this concluding chapter is to examine these goals in retrospect and ask what the Spirit has taught us through this journey of telling these stories, reflecting on their meaning for cross-cultural teamwork, and analyzing the practices described to discern possible futures for such teamwork. Let's begin with a brief restatement of those goals: (1) to identify the complex nature of wicked problems in the ministries of multinational teams, (2) to help readers discern the biblical essentials that are foundational to addressing such problems "in Christ," (3) to equip readers to detect and respond "in Christ" to six areas of "in the world" deceptions, and (4) to provide case studies of practical leadership and sacrifice that enabled teams to overcome their wicked problems and work together for the mission of God.

## "Wicked Problems": The Intractable Challenge

> The first goal is to help leaders and team members understand the
> nature of wicked problems and the inadequacy of common sense,
> routine cultural learning, past experience, and normal team dialogue
> and leadership to resolve such problems.[1]

As we saw in chapters 4 through 9, the complexity of wicked
problems—conflicting values and contested processes so necessarily
opposed—can never be wholly resolved, and for this we may lament.
To reflect briefly on the five case studies in this book, the stories are
about the most intimate contexts of team meeting, the more complex contexts of team training, and the most complex situations of
local and national ministry. The time frame for resolution or remis-
sion of such problems varies from several months to several years to
never—since the complexity may be unremitting because of ministry
expansion and change of team members. The cultural differences are
as vast as the nations and the people groups within those nations,
and the personality differences are as complex as the personalities
encountered in any village or local church. Each case also illustrates a
unique ministry challenge. At every level of ministry, wicked problems
raise their ugly heads, and without Christ, we are helpless to resolve
them or even to overcome them for a limited time.

Further, the work of the deceiver, the ancient serpent—Satan—
never stops. Satan uses our national origins to divide us, distorts
our understanding of Scripture to undermine God's message for us,
and employs our self-representation—being wealthy and needing
nothing—to foster either domination on our part or the resistance of
others in our relationships. Satan's work is global: the wealth of the
West is one of the tools for distortion and deception that he uses to
oppose the gospel and the church in every region and nation.

Each contributor has acknowledged and accepted the "wicked
problem" challenges inherent to "mission with" the nations, as well
as the unique opportunity to partner with God to equip and deploy
gifted men and women from every nation and culture for ministry.

1. From the preface (see p. xiii).

All, in their particular web of relationships, modeled and encouraged values of respect, honor, submission, and service reciprocally so as to empower all team members to exercise their gifts.

## Biblical Essentials for Cross-Cultural Teamwork

The second goal is to guide readers to biblical essentials that are foundational for leaders and team members who are from radically diverse backgrounds but seek to engage in teamwork cross-culturally "in Christ."[2]

We began this book by documenting from Paul's Epistle to the Galatians that wicked problems have plagued the church from its very beginning. From the day of Pentecost, when the Holy Spirit enabled each person present to hear the gospel in his or her own language, God used a small group of 120 Jewish believers to proclaim Christ to peoples of diverse languages and cultures. As Paul documents, gentile converts soon joined them in God's mission. In his epistles, Paul describes the following as essentials for teamwork in Christ: (1) mission in weakness—centered on the cross of Jesus; (2) identity centered in Christ, *not* in the world; (3) relationships as one body within households of faith; and (4) household life as the work of faith, the labor of love, and steadfast hope. We have examined each case study in this book with reference to these biblical essentials for "mission with" members of the body of Christ from diverse nations and cultures.

The challenge for such multinational, cross-cultural teamwork is that believers conduct themselves as "worthy of the gospel" (Phil. 1:27) and "worthy of God" (1 Thess. 2:12). But as Sue Russell reminds us, we remain in the world and therefore under continuous pressure to conform to structures of power, systems of economy, expectations for behavior, and values and priorities. Our hope must be focused on Christ so that our relationships—composed of "in the world" statuses—may be transformed to produce teams that focus on mutuality and solidarity

2. From the preface (see p. xiii).

rather than competition, domination, and honor.[3] To conduct ourselves as "worthy" is to embrace and live out in Christ the metaphors of leadership—*shepherd, servant, steward*—and of community—*one body, a household of faith*, and *the temple of God*.

What have we learned on this journey of reflection? The critical insight from all five cases is that such challenges are overcome only in Christ through the work of faith, the labor of love, and steadfast hope. In his Letter to the Colossians, Paul shows clearly the spiritual interrelationship of the triad: "the faith and love *that spring from the hope* stored up for you in heaven and about which you have already heard in the true message of the gospel" (1:5). "Christ in you, the hope of glory" (1:27) is the mystery that has been revealed in the gospel. The work of faith is "the orientation toward Christ" (Phil. 1:27) in everything that we think and do. The labor of love is "the orientation toward fellow believers" in what Paul describes as the "kingdom of the Son he loves" (Col. 1:13).[4]

As young Christians, we often do not know how to do either the work of faith or the labor of love, so we need others in the body of Christ to coach us. For example, mature mission leaders in SIM coached Penny Bakewell on how to become a shepherd and do the labor of love in her relationships with her people. Robert and Elizabeth McLean with Global Pentecostal Mission were coached, and then given the assignment to coach others, on how to serve in a household of faith engaged in mission to nonbelievers in Central Asia. The leaders in our case studies all practiced the work of faith, the labor of love, and commitments of steadfast hope in the midst of their wicked problems.

### Discerning "in the World" Deceptions and Responses

The third goal of this book is to equip readers to discern and respond "in Christ" to six areas of "in the world" deceptions that challenge leaders and team members.[5]

---

3. Russell, *In the World but Not of the World*, 156.
4. Thompson, *Apostle of Persuasion*, 222.
5. From the preface (see p. xiii).

Three of the chapters in part 2 addressed the organizational challenges of wicked problems—management, problem solving, and return on investment. Julie Green, given management responsibility and directed to work with team members to create a ministry proposal, documented how the personal biases about power and authority among her team members and the leaders of their sponsoring organization (SIL) undermined every discussion and every attempt on her part to bring them together in unity. Members contested SIL's right even to participate in the conversation and Julie's authority to lead them. These biases inhibited every attempt on her part to achieve a solution. By way of comparison, the personal biases of organizational leaders, team leaders, and team members contributed in significant ways to the wicked problems described in every case study in the book.

In addition, Julie's team fractured still further as each member insisted on "my way" of defining the problem and working toward a solution. Julie noted that their responses surprised her and confounded her attempts to put a solution on the table for discussion. Surprise was a common theme among leaders and team members in these stories. Team members in Papua New Guinea were surprised at the large differences between Westerners and Melanesians when Matthew Crosland presented the results of his value research. Penny Bakewell was surprised at the responses of North East Indian members in awe of her British identity and at the Korean member's response to her role as director. And in each case, surprise affected both leader and team perceptions of how to work toward a solution to their problem.

Julie's leadership challenge was how to confront the people on her team with the uncomfortable knowledge that separation and going one's own way was not God's purpose for the members or for their organization—a problem shared by the leaders in all five case studies. All of these teams, as members of the body of Christ, had a mission that in the end was utterly dependent on God's power and blessing. Further, unity in Christ's body was not optional, and so they had much work to do: in fact, a labor of love for one another.

Finally, SIL, SIM, Global Pentecostal Mission, and Zion World Prayer and Missions pressured their team leaders with accountability

for "returns on investment" of their ministry work, in spite of the
fact that there is little, if any, biblical ground for those demands.
Counting converts, churches, disciples, and Bibles is a cultural way
of measuring success, but—as we saw in chapter 6—God is Lord
of the harvest. Christian organizations use business language and
models to measure "profits" through the work of teams, in spite of
our understanding that what God requires is the fruit of the Spirit in
our working relationships with one another and our gospel witness.

The last three chapters in part 2 focused on issues of interpersonal
relationships—values conflicts, personality needs or hungers, and
spiritual self-deception. Chapter 7 explored the cultural and interpersonal roots of disagreement among teammates and compared data
from two very different households of faith. Bakewell's "occasional
team"—scattered widely within the nation of Ghana—gathered
three or four times a year for strategic planning meetings; Crosland's
"intensive team"—local SIL members and scattered Melanesians—
gathered for a one-week experimental course followed by two weeks
of intensive debriefing and curricular planning. In spite of the teams'
vastly different agendas and time and space relationships, both leaders discovered the strategy and value of creating *reflective space for
listening and learning* with team members.

Both leaders devised a plan of research through which they sought
to uncover whatever might hinder or help their people as they worked
toward unity of purpose. Bakewell conducted ethnographic interviews with all her team members, learning their personal histories,
their values about "following," and the source of their reluctance
to participate. Crosland developed objective exercises for reflection
(value card sorts, short stories) from which he discovered similarities
and differences in the way the SIL and Melanesian members of his
team understood time, work, and decision-making. These particular
case studies illustrate how different kinds of research may provide
a pathway for leaders to lead toward unity among team members.

Chapter 8 focused on the tensions that surfaced within teams
regarding personal identity and roles. After the initial excitement of
entering a new culture and forming a new team for ministry with
people strangely different from oneself, individuals inevitably ask,

"Why am I here, and what is my role on the team?" We assume that most people commit to such a team because they want to make a difference in the world, but some may be driven internally by a hunger for authority and significance. These emotional needs erupt during times of tension and disagreement about even minor concerns, adding fuel to the fires of disagreement. The McLeans found that these emotional undercurrents disrupted normal team relations and, when untended, had the potential to destroy personal and team relationships.

While the Ghana and Central Asia households of faith were culturally very different, their leaders shared a commitment to address the challenges of leadership through the biblical metaphors of shepherd and servant. Regarding the issue of significance (why am I here), these leaders made deep relational commitments to team members, nurturing them and guiding them toward a deeper grasp of their identity in Christ and their value and significance as members of his body serving as a team. Regarding the question of authority (what is a team and what is my role in it), these leaders modeled a new image: leaders as humble learners and vulnerable servants, empowering individuals to use their gifts for the good of the team and the mission of Christ. The contribution of these case studies is that, in Christ, the labor of love is to practice kindness, humility, and readiness to serve one another for the mission of God, turning upside down the authority and significance of title, structure, and role in the world.

Chapter 9 examined the issue of balancing our personal convictions and rights with our love for Christ and team members. Most, if not all, human beings have convictions about their identity and about their rights. When we are convinced that we are right and good, these convictions lead us to reject others who differ and even to abuse them. With identities rooted in colonialism in Africa and imperialism in the Americas, individuals on teams in Africa and Central Asia either rejected each other or felt resentment toward one another because of past political and cultural patterns of domination in the societies of team members. Old wounds and personal convictions—"I am right and good"—that team members brought with them became sources of resistance or "righteous" rejection. Atanda and the

McLeans understood that change could happen only through prayer, repentance, and embracing and empowering others.

The challenge for followers—members of teams—is repentance. When one is convinced that "I" deserve certain rights and respect, then one acts out of that conviction; but when one is convinced that one's identity is in Christ, then one acts in light of the calling to take up a cross and follow. At this point, it is possible to repent, rejecting "my rights" and recovering "my first love" in Christ. Only then are team members truly "followers" and able to embrace those who are different.

### Leadership and Sacrifice?

> The fourth goal is to provide readers with practical, twenty-first-century case studies that answer the question: What kind of leadership and sacrifice will serve teams to enable them to bring the gospel to the nations today?[6]

What have we learned? First, the common social patterns of leadership in the world are easily corrupted. Regardless of which of the four prototypical frames of leadership we endorse—authority rule, corporate rule, consensus rule, or influence rule (see chap. 14)—each fails to meet the challenges inherent in wicked problems. Julie reminded us in chapter 4 that leaders in every different way of life attempt to control through the use of authority and power. In the quest for control, we inevitably distort and quench both the Spirit of God and our working relationships with people.

Second, a quick review of our five cases provided evidence that in each a few people questioned God's appointed leaders and some hungered to take the role. In the Central Asia and West Africa cases, those with a hunger to lead also used their authority in ways that served their personal interests and goals. Given that many hunger to be a leader, God often chooses those, such as Moses and David, who declare themselves incapable of assuming such a role.

6. From the preface (see p. xiv).

What kind of leadership will serve multinational teams to enable them to bring the gospel to the nations in spite of wicked problems? In the five case studies, we discovered that our authors—Julie Green, Penny Bakewell, Robert and Elizabeth McLean, Matthew Crosland, and Martins Atanda—served with humility in their callings, gave sacrificially to team members in their practice and living, and esteemed the members of their teams as worthy servants of the Lord Jesus Christ. They did not claim these attributes for themselves; rather, each manifested these characteristics in actions appropriate to the particular wicked problem he or she faced. Bakewell invested hours of listening and dialogue to gain knowledge of the personal histories and values of her team members, and she showed her respect for them in her report. Julie Green loved her team members enough to spend months listening to them, learning from them, analyzing their feedback, and representing their views fairly to her supervisors in SIL. In Elizabeth McLean's personal reflections, she embraced her calling in Christ to love those who resisted the teaching and team strategies of Global Pentecostal Mission, and she forgave them when they criticized, resisted, and even rejected the McLeans' leadership.

Robert McLean and Matthew Crosland, both of whom were directors of curriculum and training for their organizations, demonstrated servant leadership, serving even the most resistant in their respective ministries. Crosland, a "middle manager" in SIL-PNG, gave his time for weeks of deep listening, analysis, and reflection on the values, patterns of learning, and patterns of work of expatriate SIL missionaries and Melanesian translation workers. Robert McLean spent hours building relationships and partnering with new missionaries to enable them to learn and to support their teams to become viable. Each sacrificed time and resources, giving all their energy and passion to empower their "mission recruits" to succeed and to fulfill their calling in Christ. For Martins Atanda, "mission with" is his leadership strategy—he is a shepherd inviting people to follow him into villages, towns, states, and nations; he is a servant who leads by inviting "any who will come" to a sacrificial offering of prayer to God and fasting and by giving his personal resources—food, clothing, fellowship—to support the poorest in ministry.

What practical insights can we glean from these stories that may be common strategies for "mission with"? The six authors of the case studies in this book made the following commitments:

1. They were obedient to their calling to *lead in Christ*. Their work of faith focused on Jesus, his teaching, his ministry, and his instructions for life and service. For them, following Jesus meant obeying him and doing the things he called them to do.

2. The definition of *righteousness* is having a right relationship with God and then with those in his body. These men and women had a hunger and thirst for right relationships with God, with the members of their teams, and with the people they served.

3. There is *no single pathway* to resolve or even pause the internal tensions and conflicts that are inevitable when people from diverse nations and cultures commit to work together. Every situation is made uniquely complex by the people who are involved—people with diverse backgrounds, diverse spiritual gifts, and unpredictable patterns of individual emotions and reasoning, all contributing to how they exercise their gifts in obedience to the Lord Jesus Christ.

Teams always include some who question, others who are certain that their way is the right and only way, and still others who wish to bring unity and harmony but despair when they cannot do it. And everyone is on a journey with Christ: some are deeply engaged with Christ and open and sensitive to the leading of the Holy Spirit, others are on a journey of partial or incomplete submission, and still others have signed up for the work but don't know the power of Christ in their lives. The leadership challenge is to engage in Christ and learn as one goes what it means to sacrifice, suffer, and lead in the way of the cross.

Finally, Julie has given us some basic principles that are foundational for leaders in this challenging ministry of working with multinational teams:

1. *Listening to and learning from members* is critical and must be done repeatedly, and (as Crosland found) even systematically, to discern what, why, and how the team must work together to resolve the conflict of the moment and the conflict of the season.

2. *Surprise* is a clear signal that we must listen more deeply and probe more directly into the information or perspective that has surprised us.

3. *Recognizing and applying uncomfortable knowledge*, gained in one's research into the interpersonal dynamics within a team and into the critical issues before them, is crucial for leadership. A leader must first discern what knowledge and information is uncomfortable for members of the team and then prayerfully consider how best to confront the team members with that knowledge in order to help them move forward.

4. *Discerning a process and leading collaboration* that brings team members into shared planning and decision-making is the work of "redeemed power," as illustrated by using one's authority to keep people working, defining the issues, drawing attention to tough questions, bringing volatile value differences to the surface, giving people responsibilities, protecting the weak, and pacing the work.

## "Mission with" Steadfast Hope

The resources in these five case studies provide a wealth of wisdom and guidance, if we are only willing to listen and learn before we engage in the work of faith and the labor of love with steadfast hope. But in our own strength, we cannot succeed. As we have stated repeatedly, there are only *clumsy* and *temporary* solutions to wicked problems.

So, you may ask, is all this worth it? Why should I endure so much pain and suffering to join a multinational team?

Who told you that following Jesus would be easy? Who promised you a good life, with all questions resolved in elegant and simple ways? Did God *really mean* that we should endure such misery and frustration? (I think I heard this question before, in the garden of Eden.) If you are looking for the easy way in mission, or if you are looking to be in control, you may choose that pathway of control.

But we have at our door the most powerful person who ever lived—our Lord Jesus Christ—who wants to join us on our journey. He has promised us daily guidance by the Holy Spirit and has taught us to pray and to wait. He has given us, through the Scriptures, the words of his teaching when he walked in Galilee and Judea. And—best of all—we are not alone! He has promised that when we obey his Word and commit—as members of his global church—to work with one another for his mission of witness, he will never leave us or forsake us. In our *mission from weakness*, Jesus demonstrates his strength and love. We may share in this glory with the members of his "body," the church, and they may in fact help us discover our spiritual and cultural blindness and open our eyes to things we cannot see or have somehow missed.

All the stories in this book are about people upon whom God poured out his Spirit, to whom he gave the hope of glory, and whom he led into the practice of living as a household of faith. They suffered together, sacrificed together, and witnessed together in the steadfast hope that God would lead them into his harvest and would work in them and through them to bring "good news" to the poor, sick, oppressed, and hopeless people in the nations. As they experienced the love of God in these households of faith, they were moved to share that love with others, and the Spirit of God continued to pour out the love of Christ on all who would hear.

We conclude that it is through serving and suffering with one another in Christ that we forge teams and that we are able to work as multinational teams cross-culturally. In every case, the power that keeps people loving, working, and witnessing together is God—Father, Son, and Holy Spirit—and God alone brings forth fruit. Jesus invites us to resist the deceptions of that ancient serpent, Satan; to flee the temptations that overwhelm us "in the world"; and to open our hearts and ministry to him: "Here I am! I stand at the door and knock. If anyone hears my voice and opens the door, I will come in and eat with that person, and they with me. To the one who is victorious, I will give the right to sit with me on my throne, just as I was victorious and sat down with my Father on his throne. Whoever has ears, let them hear what the Spirit says to the churches" (Rev. 3:20–22).

# Bibliography

Bazzell, Pascal D. "Who Is Our Cornelius? Learning from Fruitful Encounters at the Boundaries of Mission." In *The State of Missiology Today: Global Innovations in Christian Witness*, edited by Charles E. Van Engen, 107–24. Downers Grove, IL: InterVarsity, 2016.

Bremner, David. *Images of Leadership: Biblical Portraits of Godly Leaders.* Chicago: Oasis International, 2021.

Crosland, Matthew E. "Language Program Planning: A Culturally Appropriate Model." DIS diss., Fuller Theological Seminary, School of Intercultural Studies, 2018.

Crouch, Andy. *Strong and Weak: Embracing a Life of Love, Risk, and True Flourishing.* Downers Grove, IL: IVP Books, 2016.

Deiros, Pablo A. "Eschatology and Mission: A Latin American Perspective." In *The State of Missiology Today: Global Innovations in Christian Witness*, edited by Charles E. Van Engen, 267–84. Downers Grove, IL: InterVarsity, 2016.

Dierck, Lorraine Wendy. "Leadership and Patron-Client Structures in Thailand." In *Devoted to Christ: Missiological Reflections*, edited by Christopher L. Flanders, 106–18. Eugene, OR: Pickwick, 2019.

Goodrich, Richelle E. *Slaying Dragons: Quotes, Poetry, and a Few Short Stories for Every Day of the Year.* Self-published, CreateSpace, 2017.

Gorse, Christopher, Iain McKinney, Anthony Shepherd, and Paul Whitehead. "Meetings: Factors That Affect Group Interaction and Performance." In *Proceedings 22nd Annual ARCOM Conference, 4–6 September 2006,* edited by David Boyd, 915–24. Birmingham, UK: Association of Researchers in Construction Management, 2006.

Grint, Keith. "Problems, Problems, Problems: The Social Construction of Leadership." *Human Relations* 58, no. 11 (2005): 1467–94.

———. "Wicked Problems and Clumsy Solutions: The Role of Leadership." In *The New Public Leadership Challenge*, edited by Stephen Brookes and Keith Grint, 169–86. New York: Palgrave Macmillan, 2010.

Hibbert, Evelyn, and Richard Hibbert. *Leading Multicultural Teams*. Pasadena, CA: William Carey Library, 2014.

Hofstede, Geert H., Gert Jan Hofstede, and Michael Minkov. *Cultures and Organizations: Software of the Mind*. 3rd ed. New York: McGraw Hill, 2010.

Jenkins, Philip. *The Next Christendom: The Coming of Global Christianity*. 3rd ed. Oxford: Oxford University Press, 2011.

Jeong, Paul Yonggap. "The Essence of Leadership: Mission from a Position of Weakness." In *Devoted to Christ: Missiological Reflections*, edited by Christopher L. Flanders, 119–29. Eugene, OR: Pickwick, 2019.

Johnson, Barry. *Polarity Management: A Summary Introduction*. Middleville, MI: Polarity Management Associates, 2005. Available at https://rise-leaders.com/wp-content/uploads/2019/07/Polarity-Management-Summary-Introduction.pdf.

Koeshall, Anita. "Navigating Power." In *Devoted to Christ: Missiological Reflections*, edited by Christopher L. Flanders, 65–78. Eugene, OR: Pickwick, 2019.

Lewis, C. S. *The Screwtape Letters*. Uhrichsville, OH: Barbour, 1990.

Linder, Johan. *Working in Multicultural Teams: A Biblical and Practical Guide for Team Leaders and Members*. Sydney: Hudson, 2016.

Lingenfelter, Sherwood G. *Leadership in the Way of the Cross*. Eugene, OR: Cascade Books, 2018.

———. *Leading Cross-Culturally: Covenant Relationships for Effective Christian Leadership*. Grand Rapids: Baker Academic, 2008.

———. *Transforming Culture: A Challenge for Christian Mission*. Grand Rapids: Baker Academic, 1998.

Meyer, Erin. *The Culture Map: Breaking Through the Invisible Boundaries of Global Business*. New York: Public Affairs, 2014.

Newbigin, Lesslie. *The Open Secret: An Introduction to Theology of Mission*. Grand Rapids: Eerdmans, 1995.

Parks, Sharon Daloz. *Leadership Can Be Taught*. Boston: Harvard Business School, 2005.

Plueddemann, James E. *Leading across Cultures: Effective Ministry and Mission in the Global Church*. Downers Grove, IL: InterVarsity, 2009.

Rayner, Steve. "Uncomfortable Knowledge: The Social Construction of Ignorance in Science and Environmental Policy Discourses." *Economy and Society* 41, no. 1 (2012): 107–25.

Reisacher, Evelyne. *Joyful Witness in the Muslim World: Sharing the Gospel in Everyday Encounters*. Grand Rapids: Baker Academic, 2016.

Russell, A. Sue. *In the World but Not of the World: The Liminal Life of Pre-Constantine Christian Communities*. Eugene, OR: Pickwick, 2019.

Silzer, Sheryl Takagi. *Biblical Multicultural Teams*. Pasadena, CA: William Carey Library, 2011.

Thompson, James W. *Apostle of Persuasion: Theology and Rhetoric in the Pauline Letters*. Grand Rapids: Baker Academic, 2020.

Thompson, Michael, Richard Ellis, and Aaron B. Wildavsky. *Cultural Theory, Political Cultures*. Boulder, CO: Westview, 1990.

Tonstad, Sigve K. *Revelation*. Grand Rapids: Baker Academic, 2020.

Tuckman, Bruce W. "Developmental Sequence in Small Groups." *Psychological Bulletin* 63, no. 6 (1965): 384–99.

# Contributors

**Martins Atanda (Odutola Adewole)**, founding director, Zion World Prayer and Missions, Nigeria

**Penny Bakewell**, area director, SIM International, Ghana

**Matthew E. Crosland**, academic training manager, SIL-PNG, and principal, Pacific Institute of Languages, Arts and Translation (PILAT), 2014–2020

**Julie A. Green**, international anthropology coordinator, SIL International, 2010–2020

**Sherwood G. Lingenfelter**, senior professor of anthropology, provost emeritus, Fuller Theological Seminary

**Elizabeth McLean** (pseudonym), codirector of training, Global Pentecostal Mission, Central Asia

**Robert McLean** (pseudonym), area director, Global Pentecostal Mission, Central Asia

# Index